RETHINK HAPPY

Praise for **Rethink Happy**

"Scaling up a business not only takes its toll on the owner; it tends to spill over onto the family and other personal relationships, often ending in tragic messes. But it doesn't need to be this way. We like to say that "routine sets you free"— and Doug's book brilliantly highlights those routines that will set you free, bringing joy to both your life and those around you. It just requires the same skills needed to grow a successful business—focus and discipline."

—**Verne Harnish**, CEO Gazelles and author of
Scaling Up (Rockefeller Habits 2.0)

"Recent high profile business disasters have reminded us that intellect, degrees and 80 hour weeks are not the essential ingredients for business success. In a delightful story form **Rethink Happy** captures the soul of business and reminds us that uncompromising character, respectful relationships and a commitment to the greater good of community lead to "uncommon" success and a life worth living."

—**Dan Miller**, author *48 Days to the Work You Love*

"**Rethink Happy** is a wonderful surprise. Like any allegory, it takes the reader on the same journey as the protagonist, but most such stories telegraph the lesson long before the character in the book figures it out. Kisgen's writing brings you along at the same speed, and with the same pleasure of discovery. Anyone who wonders why success in business is never…quite…enough owes this book to themselves!"

—**John Dini**, author *Hunting in a Farmer's World*

"Doug's book applies old-school philosophy with new-school science and wraps it into an engaging narrative that keeps the pages turning. And your mind thinking! ***Rethink Happy*** will do just what the title suggests: cause you to rethink how to achieve authentic joy. A must read for all business owners and entrepreneurs!"

—**Ford Saeks**, CEO Prime Concepts Group Inc.

"Rethink Happy serves as a poignant reminder that it's easy to succumb to self-centeredness, but in the end, the happiest people are those who live to serve others."

—**Paul Hogan**, Chairman and Founder,
Home Instead Senior Care

"Original and entertaining, ***Rethink Happy*** offers down-to-earth self-discovery lessons through a light-hearted, purposeful story."

—**Mary Leonida**, President and CEO,
Polaris Cos. and Track Consulting

"Everyone loses their way on their journey from time-to-time. Moreover, we struggle with the first steps to get us on the right path. ***Rethink Happy*** provides simple directions to find great joy in life for you and those you encounter on your journey in a compelling tale of mentorship."

—**Tim Opsitnick**, Founder, JURINNOV Ltd.

"Prepare to be inspired! Yes, each one of us is called to live a more authentic and meaningful life."

—**John S. Archer**, President & CEO,
Concepts for Business, LLC

"Doug's book describes real-life situations that not only entrepreneurs and successful people struggle with. Many people are chasing the American dream without realizing what really matters in order to live a joyful life. *Rethink Happy* shows you what's truly important with a style, chapter format and characters that will keep you wanting to read more. "

—**Shawn George**, President, Elite Lighting Designs, Inc.

RETHINK
HAPPY

An Entrepreneur's Journey Toward
AUTHENTIC JOY

Doug Kisgen

New York

RETHINK HAPPY

An Entrepreneur's Journey Toward AUTHENTIC JOY

© 2016 Doug Kisgen.

All rights reserved. No portion of this book may be reproduced, stored in a retrieval system, or transmitted in any form or by any means—electronic, mechanical, photocopy, recording, scanning, or other—except for brief quotations in critical reviews or articles, without the prior written permission of the publisher.

Published in New York, New York, by Morgan James Publishing. Morgan James and The Entrepreneurial Publisher are trademarks of Morgan James, LLC.
www.MorganJamesPublishing.com

The Morgan James Speakers Group can bring authors to your live event. For more information or to book an event visit The Morgan James Speakers Group at
www.TheMorganJamesSpeakersGroup.com.

Shelfie

A **free** eBook edition is available with the purchase of this print book.

CLEARLY PRINT YOUR NAME ABOVE IN UPPER CASE

Instructions to claim your free eBook edition:
1. Download the Shelfie app for Android or iOS
2. Write your name in **UPPER CASE** above
3. Use the Shelfie app to submit a photo
4. Download your eBook to any device

ISBN 978-1-63047-734-9 paperback
ISBN 978-1-63047-735-6 eBook
Library of Congress Control Number:
2015913307

Cover Design by:
Rachel Lopez
www.r2cdesign.com

Interior Design by:
Bonnie Bushman
The Whole Caboodle Graphic Design

In an effort to support local communities and raise awareness and funds, Morgan James Publishing donates a percentage of all book sales for the life of each book to Habitat for Humanity Peninsula and Greater Williamsburg

Get involved today, visit
www.MorganJamesBuilds.com

Habitat
for Humanity®
Peninsula and
Greater Williamsburg
Building Partner

To my wife and soul mate, Kate,
and our children,
Cass, Al, Joe, Liv, and Thomas.

TABLE OF CONTENTS

Chapter 1

SHADOW

I can't believe I've gotten myself into this mess. Why am I going to all this effort if I'm getting nothing from it? Why'd Camino have to pick me, of all the people at the game, to sit by that day? I was fine. Just fine. I was successful, had a place I felt at home, even though it was at Ted's bar and ironically, not at home. I was a good father—I mean, I provided for my kids and I didn't demand a lot from my wife.

The twinge of guilt was like an arrow to my heart, from out of nowhere, as I remembered my son's reaction last night when I tried Camino's suggestion to "shoot the breeze" with him. Did I really only want to talk to him when I was pointing out something he was doing wrong?

And my wife thought I came home "early" last night, even though it was a good two hours after I left the office. Okay, so maybe I'm not going to get Father of the Year or the Husband Achievement Award, but my kids get pretty much everything they want and my wife can go shopping anytime.

I was just thinking about that at the game the other day. I've got it pretty good. I mean, things could always improve, right? What was it I was daydreaming about that day? Before Camino pushed his way into my life? Oh yeah, I was thinking about the trip I'd canceled with my son. Again. Ah yes, there's that familiar feeling of failure now. I wasn't even watching the game, and suddenly I'd felt a presence.

A shadow fell over me, blocking the sun. As I wasn't seated within peanut-throwing distance of anyone else, naturally I looked up to see who could be blocking my sun. The tall stranger didn't say a word. Just took a seat (*c'mon man!*) right next to me.

Okay, just ignore him. Don't let anybody spoil this time. It's me time! C'mon, Cleve. Back to the smell of the grass, the taste of the cold beer in your hand. This is the life! Am I right? I'm free to do this—that's the American dream, right?

Chapter 2

THE INTRODUCTION

Out of the corner of my eye, I noticed he was watching me out of the corner of his. *Dang it, Cleve. You know the first rule: Never make eye contact.* I nodded. He nodded back. *Well, this is just going swimmingly. Can I just ignore him now?* Sighing, I leaned forward, hoping to avoid any conversation.

Apparently he felt the same way, because he leaned forward too, as though to better grasp the situation on the diamond. I relaxed a bit. Maybe I really could get through this.

"So, what do you think?" The question came out of nowhere. I glanced at him again.

"Excuse me?" I was trying my best not to be rude, but man, he sat right next to me in a section full of empty seats. This was "me" time and it was sacred.

"I said, 'What do you think?'" He was facing me now. *Uh-oh, this does not look good.* I tried to pay attention at the crack of the bat. As one of the players made his way to first base, I sighed.

"I heard you the first time," I answered. The grit in my response should have been enough to scare off most strangers.

"Well then, what do you think?" He asked me again.

Suddenly, I noticed his piercing blue eyes. It felt like they were looking deep into my soul. I broke eye contact. *This is ridiculous. Get a grip, man!*

"What do I think about the game?" I took a stab, hoping he was going for light conversation, although I felt like I already knew this wasn't going to be about our team's dismal record.

"Well, sure, I guess we can talk about that for a minute," he responded, extending his hand. "I'm Camino."

"Camino? Like the El Camino car?" I held back a laugh, but it was tough. All I could think about was how ugly those things were! The businessman in me had me attempting politeness, but the real me was begging to head for the concession stands to get another beer and find another seat.

Fine. I'll be polite. "Cleve," I said, taking his hand. It was a firm grasp, which I appreciated. No "limp fish" grip here. My respect rose a notch, but my interest was still at a flat zero.

"Cleve? Like Cleveland?" Camino was looking at me with a glint of laughter in his eyes. "Your parents big fans of one of the teams?"

"Nope, they're actually Grover Cleveland fans," I said, a bit sharply. "It may not be the coolest name, but at least I wasn't named after a blue Muppet!"

Camino chuckled, and it wasn't an altogether unpleasant sound. "I hear ya."

I couldn't help myself. "Okay, so I've never met anybody named Camino before. Where did that come from?" *Why am I encouraging him? I should be paying attention to the fact that my team is on the ropes, and they're making a run in the eighth inning!*

"It's a long story," Camino said mysteriously. "I'll tell you all about it sometime, but for now, let's enjoy what we have in common."

"What's that?" I know, I know, I was still encouraging him, but now I was curious.

"Baseball," Camino said simply. For some reason, I felt like he'd been about to share some dark secret that only I knew. I was relieved and yet oddly disappointed in the simplicity of his answer.

"Oh, yeah," I responded, leaning back on the empty bleacher behind me. *Okay, Cleve, back to the game. Bottom of the eighth, and the tying run is at the plate.*

We sat in comfortable silence for the next few moments, breaking it only to yell when the ball headed for the outfield and sigh when it ended in a disappointing out. It's hard to put into words how I felt during the ninth inning as we cheered together and otherwise enjoyed the silence.

Most people make me feel sort of uncomfortable, but I realized that after those first few moments of annoyance, Camino wasn't one of them. Strange. At first I'd been annoyed that he'd chosen to sit by me. Now it seemed okay. Almost pleasant. Almost.

Chapter 3

THE INVITE

W ell, another day, another loss," I said. "Not that I'm surprised, but for awhile there, I thought we had a good chance of winning this one." After all, we were the worst team in the league.

"Losing still hurts, even when it's expected," Camino said wisely as we headed up the stairs.

"Yeah, I guess," I agreed. "But the good thing about losing is it keeps the seats fairly empty. Usually I don't have to rub shoulders with anybody." Suddenly I realized I'd just insulted Camino.

"I uh, I didn't mean," I stammered. I was sure my face was beet red. *Way to make a great impression!*

Camino turned, putting a hand on my shoulder. "It's okay," he grinned. "I know what you mean. Usually I don't bother people at the game."

"Well, you must be pretty die-hard to come at all when you know they're going to lose, right?" I was feeling a little better now, but still embarrassed at what I'd said to Camino.

"For sure," Camino answered, turning to head toward the exit again.

"Then why haven't I seen you at a game before?" I was curious, and darn it, I had to ask the question.

"Actually, this is the first game I've ever been to," Camino admitted. "I've always watched the games from home, but today I had a special reason for coming."

"Oh yeah, what's that?" I cringed inwardly at the question. I had a strange feeling I wasn't going to like the answer.

"Well, you wouldn't believe me if I told you, and I don't have time to explain right now," Camino said as we exited toward the parking lot. "I have to get back to work. And so do you, I imagine?"

Why the guilt, Cleve? I couldn't explain why I suddenly was a bit sad, but his question seemed innocent enough.

"Yes, I need to check in real quick before I call it a day," I said, avoiding his piercing gaze.

"Here's my card, Cleve," Camino said, handing me a small white business card. "Why don't you give me a call and we can meet for lunch sometime this week? I have a few tips

I want to share with you. It might just help you do what you do a little better."

"Excuse me?" Now my back was up. How did he know what I do? "I do just fine."

"Hold on now, don't get all bent out of shape," Camino said gently, his hands held palms out as if I were pointing a gun at him.

"Well how do you know what I do?" I was a little more annoyed now.

"First of all, the things I want to share with you are ideas and tips that can help everyone do better in whatever they are doing," Camino began. "For some, I can help them even more."

"I don't want any," I snapped.

"Tips?" Camino showed surprise for the first time.

"Whatever it is you're selling, I don't want any," I said. I shook my head, disgusted with myself for falling even this far for a sales trick. I'm a salesman—I should know better.

"Not selling anything, Cleve," Camino said calmly. "I figure you're in sales or you own your own business or something. Am I right?"

"C'mon, man," I bit the words off as I shifted from one foot to another, suddenly anxious to be done with this whole thing.

"Just answer the question," Camino requested, still apparently not fazed by my snappy retorts.

"Yes, I own my own business, and yes, I too, am in sales," I threw back at him.

"Okay, so what I have to share will take your sales to the next level," Camino shared. "I mean, I know you must be doing okay or you couldn't afford to take an afternoon off at the ballpark, right?"

"I do okay." I'm allowed one white lie, right? *At least I didn't say I was doing great. How does he know all this?* My "you-know-what" meter was still going off, but I needed to remember my manners.

"Alright, well think about it," Camino said. "And give me a call when you want to know more. It was nice to meet you, Cleve."

Then the man just turned and walked off. Just like that! I was still having a hard time grasping the whole thing. Minding my own business, enter stranger. Strikes up unwanted conversation; then asks me to go to lunch. Weird. And all his card said was "Camino," and under that was a phone number.

Very weird. The whole encounter seemed surreal, and I still wasn't sure he wasn't selling something. But there wasn't a doubt in my mind whether I would call him or not.

Chapter 4

CHECK-IN

The rest of the day was a blur, but I did trudge back to work. After a quick hello to my receptionist, I headed for my posh corner office. Ha. Honestly, it's a measly desk in an unfurnished room and there's no window in sight. I mean, I didn't need a window—I owned a manufacturing company, for crying out loud.

Frankly though, I couldn't afford it anyway, and I'd had to sell off the things I did have in there to make payroll a few months ago. But hey, my car is really my office, since I spend most of my time on the road selling.

We make those promotional mini-cars you see sitting at dealerships around the country. Or actually, you don't see too many these days. Dealerships aren't buying them. Times are tough. So we are seriously contemplating a pivot. Consequently, I brought in a guy I think can help. More about him later.

I checked my messages, and it looked like I didn't miss much. One of my clients was very unhappy, because evidently although we delivered a promotional car on time, it went to the wrong dealership. They had a raffle for the car and no car to raffle off. Yikes. Well, today was very draining. I clearly was not going to make that call before heading home. What I needed was a stiff drink to unwind after such a long day.

Chapter 5

CHEERS!

I probably could've just let my car take me to Ted's; since I was there so often, it probably knew the way. I pulled in beside a Porsche. A Porsche. Seriously? Phil was here too?

A pang of jealousy hit me like a tidal wave. Now *there* was a guy with a posh corner office. He even had a fish tank and a wet bar in his office. I saw it myself or I wouldn't have believed it. He had me pretend to be a big shot lawyer so I could set up a meeting with him when I said I didn't believe his office was really that nice.

Kind of made me wonder why a guy with all that has to invent a story. Sure seems to love his job though. There's a lot less pressure working for someone else. But then again, there's the whole security thing. Since I'm in charge, I know I'll have my job no matter what. Phil doesn't have that kind of security.

I tapped my fingers on the steering wheel. Did I really want to go in? Did I want to listen to Phil's stories about his latest adventure vacation or his new billion-dollar client? All for a drink? I thought about the alternative and then made my decision. Yes. Yes I did want a drink that badly.

"Hey Cleve, how ya doin'?" Ted winked in my direction as I made my way to the bar. Turns out Phil was in a booth tonight, with some slinky blonde wrapped around him. *Whew!* Yeah, that seemed to be part of the package too—a different woman every time I saw him. Gorgeous and glitzy, and obviously dying to show him affection. *Why can't Cindy be like that?*

Ted was the typical bartender. Good listener, always ready for a laugh, and a real artist when it came to mixing drinks. His vodka gimlets were just what I needed after a long day. He always added just enough lime juice to bring you close to a pucker, but not quite there. I've had one or two on occasion. Okay, more like three or four on a fairly consistent basis, but who's counting?

"Typical day at the office, Ted," I said. "Made a few calls, forced myself to catch the ball game in person, read some messages, etcetera, etcetera."

"I don't know how you do it," Ted said as he dried a beer glass. "You can go to the games, catch a drink on your way home, and still support your family. You're livin' the dream, man!"

Living the dream? I'd never really thought about it that way. I mean yeah, it's nice that I can take off and have some freedoms, but me, Cleveland Gordon, living the American dream? I doubt that, otherwise wouldn't I be happier now?

"Hey, I think we're both living the dream, my friend," I said, slapping the bar with my hand. "Look at this place. People love it and keep coming back, and you're doing something you love to do."

"Yeah, but I'd rather have a wife and kids to go home to like you do," Ted grinned as he poured my drink and topped it with a slice of lime.

"Sure," I said with a derisive chuckle.

"No, really," Ted said. "It must be nice."

Nice? Is it nice when I'm usually just irritated by my wife? Is it nice that I'm not even sure my kids like me, let alone love me? And Ted is jealous of me? I was probably going to need another drink to help make sense of that one.

"Well, ah, yeah, I guess it has its advantages," I agreed.

"No offense buddy, but I've seen your wife, and she's a pretty lady," Ted said as he went back to drying glasses.

I thought for a moment. Cindy hardly ever wore makeup anymore, unless she was going somewhere important. Or to church. *Not that you would know, since you haven't gone with her in ages.* Guilty again. Now I *knew* I was going to need another drink.

I drained the last bit and snapped it down on the bar top. "Another one, Ted."

"Sure, Cleve, comin' right up," Ted said amiably. He finished up a cosmo that I noticed was delivered to the buxom blonde nibbling on Phil's ear. *Sheesh. Get a room.* Then I realized they probably would, and suddenly, I was embarrassed at the jealousy ripping through me.

I didn't really want that life, did I? I used to be thrilled to go home to my pretty wife. When had that changed? When the kids were born? Nah, if I was honest with myself (and if I can't be honest with myself, then who can I be honest with?), it was sometime before that.

I couldn't quite put my finger on it, but as I sipped my second gimlet, I knew I had to admit that my life wasn't quite the "dream" Ted made it out to be. I'd never really spent a lot of time with my kids. Unless you count the times I was badgering them over something. But it was either spend time with them and be poor, or make the money and work late so they could have the things they wanted. And I knew they wanted stuff. They were always wanting something. Weren't they?

And maybe I didn't give my wife as much attention as she would like; but honestly, I didn't bug her during her book club meetings every month (boy, was I glad I didn't have to listen to *that*!) and I gave her a very generous shopping allowance. She cooked and cleaned, and I cut the grass. That was the deal we'd made. I couldn't remember when we'd made that deal, but it was done. She didn't ask me to help with the kids when they were little, and I didn't ask her to treat the lawn for weeds. It was more of a silent understanding.

Sometime during all this thinking, I'd reached the bottom of another drink. "Hit me, Ted," I said with a smile.

Chapter 6

DREAMS AND FIGHTS

Y ou know, maybe you'd better head home, Cleve," Ted
suggested lightly. He was clearing the glasses a waitress
had set on the bar.

I noticed Phil making his way toward the door with
the blonde and the stab of envy came again. "Nah, my wife
called me before I got here and told me to stay as long as I
want," I said. That, of course, was a lie. Was that two fibs
today now? Ah, why did I even keep track? It wasn't going to
harm anybody.

"She knows how tough it is to be a business owner," I quipped, stacking on a third lie. There I go keeping track again. Why couldn't I stop that? "A guy's got to unwind, you know."

"Man, you really are living the dream," Ted laughed. "Most guys would end up sleeping on the couch tonight if they did what you did."

"Yeah, but I'm not most guys," I winked at him. He handed me the third drink. *Or was it four?* I decided then and there, I wasn't counting lies and I wasn't counting drinks. Not tonight. I deserved to take a break. I took a strong sip. I suspected Ted used less and less alcohol with each drink he gave me, and sometimes he even called a cab for me.

I actually had lost track of how many drinks I'd had, and my head felt a bit floaty when I stood up later. But it wasn't like I hadn't done this a hundred times before. Besides, I was less than a mile from home.

"Leaving us?" Ted was wiping down the bar and eyeing me suspiciously. I'm sure he was deliberating whether I was too buzzed to drive, so I straightened my spine and made an effort to speak clearly.

"Yeah, I gotta get home in time for the big fight," I said, doing my best not to wobble.

Ted looked up in surprise. "I didn't know there was a fight on tonight!"

"Oh there is," I laughed. "It's the fight between me and my wife when I get home late after hanging out here!"

Ted laughed too, but his question caught me off guard. "I thought you said she was fine with you being here awhile?"

"Oh, she is, she is," I waved off his question as I grabbed my keys from the bar top. I scribbled my name on the check and saluted Ted before heading toward the door. "I just realized how late it was, and even Cindy has her limits. Thanks, Ted."

"You're fine to drive, Cleve?" Ted's voice was laced with concern.

"Yep, I'm good," I said, continuing my concentrated effort to reach the front door.

"Okay man, have a good one," Ted called before the door slammed behind me.

When I reached my car, I realized I didn't really want to go home yet. I put the key in the ignition but didn't turn it. For some reason, I thought about that guy. Camino. *What a dumb name.* I was giggling a bit, and I knew I needed to compose myself.

Chapter 7
THE CALL

I pulled his card from my wallet and stared at it for a minute, as if it would somehow give me insight into what the man wanted. I knew I was going to call him. I'd known it all along. I am too dang curious. I'd just go ahead and get it out of the way now.

After two rings, he answered. "Hello?" His voice sounded familiar, as if I'd known him all my life. Strange. *Must be the gimlets talking.* I held back another giggle.

"Hey, is this Camino?" Duh. Like I didn't recognize his voice.

"Yes, it is," Camino answered.

"Well, okay, um, this is Cleve, you know, from the baseball game?" I sounded stupid. Like some schoolboy calling a girl for a date. Like when I'd first called Cindy.

"Of course, Cleve, how's it going?" He was smiling, I could tell. It just sounded like it, you know? His voice had that warm tone people get when they're smiling.

"Okay, so my schedule fills up pretty fast, so I figured I'd go ahead and ink you in for lunch before I got too busy and had another appointment scheduled," I lied. Again. My schedule *rarely* filled up anymore, which is how I could get away to games.

"That would be great, Cleve," Camino answered. But he was waiting, I guess, for me to make the suggestion. So I did.

"How about Friday?"

"Friday's good," he said. Silence again. Boy, he was making me do everything! This was a lot of work for something Camino had suggested.

"Okay, how about meeting at Cliff's Café off Eighty-Seventh and Broadway at noon?" I waited, but he didn't leave me hanging.

"Sure, that sounds good, Cleve," Camino said. "Looking forward to it."

"Yeah, well, okay, me too," I said. *Me too? Really?* Hmm. When I thought about it, I realized I actually *was* looking forward to it. Why? I had no idea. "See you then."

"Yep, bye now," Camino responded before hanging up. He hung up on me? I'm usually the one to get the last word in on the phone. That was just the way I figured it should be.

Well, either I just happened to pick the right day or Camino wasn't a very busy guy. I tried to picture what he did for a living. He seemed like a jack-of-all-trades kind of guy, which usually meant master-of-none. Why was I looking forward to meeting with some strange guy? And more importantly, why in the world did he want to meet with me?

Chapter 8

HOME SWEET HOME!

oney, I'm home!" I love saying that, even though I know it's a total cliché. I'm not sure Cindy appreciates it. Actually, I'm fairly confident she doesn't appreciate it at all, especially when I come home really late like tonight.

She was a great wife, when I really thought about it. She was an excellent cook, kept the house in fairly good order, and she kept the children in line quite well. Mostly because I was no good at it.

I wanted to be their buddy. I mean, I've only got so much time with them because of my busy schedule, right? *And my late nights at Ted's.* There's that guilt again. Anyway, I want to make sure they like me. The way I look at it, the nicer you are to your kids when they're growing up, the more likely they are to come visit you when you get older. Unfortunately, the buddy system didn't seem to be working so well for me. Why could I walk in to laughter between Cindy and the kids when she was way harder on them than I was? I always felt a twinge of jealousy from the easy, familiar laughter they gave her. It didn't seem fair.

"So, did you stop by Ted's on your way home again, Cleveland?" Ouch. Yeah, the use of my full name was never a good sign. Looked like my fight joke was actually going to become reality.

"C'mon, Cindy," I started. "I've got appointment after appointment all day. Building a business is a numbers game, and you know that. I have to work hard to put this roof over our head and keep making the payments on your nice minivan in the garage."

"That doesn't answer my question," Cindy said, crossing her arms while she stared holes in me.

Truth or lie? *Tread carefully, Cleve. This is a field of landmines. She probably already knows the truth.* "Honey, you don't know what it's like to have the pressure of running your own business," I said.

She was already shaking her head and turning away from me. She finished wiping down the counter she just cleared while I continued my tap dance through the minefield.

"I need a little downtime to relax and unwind. You know that," I said matter-of-factly. "You know Ted's been there for me through some tough times." That part was actually true, at least. After our daughter was born, Cindy struggled a bit with postpartum depression, and frankly, I just couldn't handle it. Ted had been my shoulder to cry on.

That experience also taught us that two kids was enough! Neither of us wanted to go through that again. "He's a good friend, and he helps me prepare for the transition home after I've had a rough day."

"So you need a couple of stiff drinks to face your wife and kids? Is that what it is?" Her back was ramrod straight, and her head came up like a startled horse when I touched her shoulder.

"No, of course not, honey, but I don't want to dump all my troubles on you and the kids when I get home," I said. Yeah, that sounded pretty good. "So I dump it on Ted, have a drink or two, and then come home to relax with you guys."

She moved out of reach and turned to face me again. "Who helps me make the transition to you coming home?" The question stung a bit.

"Come on, Cindy, give me a break," I retorted. "What does that even mean?"

"Forget it, Cleve," she spat. "You'll never change." She threw down the dishcloth.

"Change? What would you want to change about the wonderful man you married?" I knew it was a mistake as soon as the words were out, but it was too late.

"I don't have time to start that list, and you missed dinner with the family.

Again. The kids are already in bed, and this time I didn't make you a plate. There aren't even leftovers, unless you count the broccoli. Good luck with that. I'm going to bed."

I checked my watch as she beelined for our bedroom. Nine o'clock? What adult goes to bed at this time of the evening? I knew I never should have gotten her that flat- screen for the bedroom. Oh well, at least this way I could watch sports and unwind in peace. Kick back, have a snack. Another day in the life of a guy just living the American dream.

As I munched my chips and downed a beer, I flipped channels, finally landing on the sports channel. I heard his voice and saw his lips moving, but I wasn't focused on his report at all. All I could see was the hurt in Cindy's eyes when she was battering me with questions.

Chapter 9

RUDE AWAKENING

I cannot stand the alarm clock. We go way back and it's a hate-hate relationship that involves me hitting it at least three times before I even open my eyes. I'd love to eliminate it from my life altogether, but I haven't figured out how to do that yet. The silver lining to the situation was that hearing the alarm clock meant Cindy hadn't locked me out of the bedroom last night. I didn't even remember coming to bed.

I trudged into the kitchen where my son was putting away stacks of pancakes. Cindy was nowhere to be seen.

"Mornin', Dad," Brian said through a yawn.

"Mornin', son, how's it going?" I slapped him on the shoulder as I sat next to him. I realized my coffee cup wasn't on the table as usual. Maybe Cindy was still mad.

"Pretty good," Brian said. "So, where were you last night? Mom made her famous chicken-fried chicken."

Darn. That's my favorite, and she knows it. "Well, you know, Brian, it was the usual." I began another tap dance. "The client meetings went long. I've gotta work hard if I'm going to build an empire. Speaking of working hard, how's your math grade looking? Worked it back up to a C yet?"

"Not yet, Dad." Brian's eyes bounced away from mine.

"You know darn well they're not going to let you play basketball this year if you don't have C's and above in everything," I pointed out.

"I know," Brian said, exasperation evident in his voice. "You tell me all the time, and I get it. But I've been thinking. I mean, I don't even *like* basketball."

My head snapped up. "Them's fightin' words, son," I said sternly. "Seriously though, you know basketball is your best chance for a scholarship."

"Yeah, but I don't like it as much as football."

"Who cares? If you don't get a scholarship, you won't go to college and you know it!" I was tired of his excuses. "You've got to think of your family and your future."

I shoved back from the table and grabbed a travel mug from the cabinet. "You better get things figured out or I'm going to sic your mother on you!"

I looked around, realizing I hadn't seen Cindy yet this morning. "Where is your mother, anyway?"

"She said she had to leave early for work today," Brian said.

"What? She didn't tell me," I said as I tightened the lid on my coffee. "Well, where's your sister then?"

"Mom took her in early. She has choir practice on Wednesday, don't you remember that?" Shaking his head, he took his plate to the sink.

"Oh, yeah, that's right," I said. Actually, the truth was that I didn't remember. I was a little ticked off that she hadn't reminded me about that last night.

"Fine, get your backpack and let's go." I grabbed my laptop bag. "I'm going to be late for work since I have to take you to school."

Chapter 10

SETTING AN EXAMPLE

As we climbed in the car, I was already putting on my headset so I could call the office. I needed to confirm my schedule for the day and let Sandy know I was running late.

"Sandy?" She had picked up on the first ring. "Yeah, I'm running a bit late."

"Don't forget you've got an appointment with Bill at nine," she reminded me.

"Dang it, I completely forgot about that! You could've said something yesterday, you know!" Bill was my right-hand guy and he wanted an update. Even with my little BMW M3 I wasn't going to get there fast enough after taking Brian to school in the complete opposite direction of the office.

"Tell Bill I had a minor emergency at home," I said.

"Dad, that's a lie," Brian cut in.

I ignored Brian and continued on. "But I got it taken care of and I'm on my way now, okay? Thanks." Hanging up, I cut my eyes toward Brian.

"Don't you ever interrupt me when I'm on the phone with the office," I started. "Why do I have to keep telling you things like that?" Sometimes I think he's just *trying* to make me mad. You would think the kid would be smart enough to realize that making me look bad to my employees wasn't going to help me at all.

"A lie is a lie, Dad," Brian said. And if that wasn't enough, he followed it up with a biting, "You're supposed to set a good example for me."

"Look, Brian, you have no idea how hard it is to be an adult," I answered. "Sometimes you've got to skim the truth a bit if you want to keep putting food on the table and basketball shoes on your son's feet."

"I've already said I don't even like basketball," Brian said. "And that's not the point."

I ignored him. I think if I would've said anything else, it might have been really out of line, and I didn't want him to go off to school with the word "idiot" ringing in his head.

We rode in silence until we reached his school. There wasn't another car in sight, but a few other stragglers were running in the front door as the starting bell was ringing.

"I'm late," Brian accused. "This is the third time this semester, and I'm going to get detention." He slammed the door and jogged toward the school.

I was going to have to talk to Cindy about this. The kids are her job. If she lived in my world for one day, she'd realize she shouldn't ask me to take on any of these responsibilities. She should've gotten the kids up early enough to drop them both off at their schools and get to work on time herself. Shaking my head, I cranked my little M up to see what she could do about getting me to work in a hurry.

Chapter 11
RIGHT-HAND GUY

Y ou're late," Bill said. He was sitting in my office with one ankle crossed over the other knee—the picture of sophisticated ease.

"I realize that, Bill," I said. "Sorry. I had an emergency with my son. You know how teenagers can be."

"No, actually, I don't," Bill responded tartly. Bill was on his fourth marriage. The first two wives had left him, and he'd divorced the third. The fourth had just informed him that she was "seeing other people." No children, thank goodness. No pets. Three houses, six cars, a yacht, and probably millions in the bank. Why he works for me, I still can't figure out.

He doesn't have to, but he does anyway. I mean, this guy has everything. Well, if you take away the whole relationship thing, he does. And since they all sign pre-nups, his wives get a big fat nothing when the marriages are over.

"Right, well, be thankful you haven't had the experience of trying to raise a teenager," I quipped. "It's scary stuff." Bill just cocked one eyebrow in my direction as I settled myself.

"The only thing that scares me is women," Bill said with a bit of a laugh. "I'll never figure them out, but darn it if I can't quit trying!"

My nervous laugh was somewhere in between "this is funny" and "I'm not sure if you're joking" and seemed to bring Bill to the point.

"Cleve, the reason I wanted an update is probably pretty obvious to you," Bill began. "The numbers aren't looking too great. In fact, our revenue this quarter is our lowest in two years. Are we going to make it?" He sat back, his fingers steepled in his lap while he stared me down.

I've seen that look several times over the past few years. It was his "put-up or shut-up" look, and I hated it. It made me feel less owner, more employee. But I had to admit, he was right. I knew he'd walk away from me, from the business, from everything if something didn't change.

I'm good with ideas and selling, but I'm horrible with detail and follow-through. I got to a point where I finally admitted I needed a partner to be the operations guy or I was going to tank the whole business. I'd heard of Bill long before we connected, and we had a heck of a time getting our schedules to cross.

I'd actually given up on the notion of meeting with him when one day I was at lunch with a customer and Bill was seated at the next table. Of course, I didn't know it at the time, but my customer was very familiar with him and was happy to introduce us. Next thing I know, we're running a business together. He was the glue that held my crazy ideas and my ADD personality together.

Bill wasn't privy to all of the details of our sales team. Okay, me. There. It's out there—I *am* the sales team. In this instance, there definitely is an "I" in team. So, I had a couple of options here. I could blame the economy, the production staff, the lack of innovation in our products, or I could just bite the bullet and be honest with him.

The economy option might work, but it was a tired response. He'd heard it before. The production staff was under his jurisdiction and he'd likely take offense to me pointing the blame in that direction. (Plus, it actually *wasn't* their fault.) Lack of innovation came back to me.

I was burned out. I felt stuck. I've got a mortgage, a wife and kids, payments on two cars, and there was no way I could chuck it all and start over in some other profession. Making and selling these silly little cars was all I knew. I'd been doing it since I was still wet behind the ears.

Bracing myself, I leaned back in my own chair, trying to appear in control. "Bill, I've got this," I started. "You know I do. Have I ever let you down? The economy is crap and you know it." There it was—the economy. I'll admit, it was easy to blame it on the economy.

Bill's tired look was enough to spur me on. "We're getting killed out there. Brooks and Johnson have both made several innovations in the last two years. We haven't changed a thing, but we still charge more than they do. Despite the fact that I like being higher priced, it's getting harder to sell the value without improvements."

Bill was shaking his head. "This is getting old, Cleve."

"Listen, Bill, I just haven't come up with a new pivot strategy yet, but I am getting closer," I pleaded. I knew he would leave me high and dry with no looking back if I didn't get things turned around. He looked at my company and me as a fun little pet project. But so far it hadn't been fun for either of us.

"I just need a little more time," I said. The sweat was starting to gather at the small of my back. I could feel it.

"I've given you two years, Cleve," Bill said, sitting forward now. "You've been promising to deliver for *two* years." His two fingers emphasized the length of time.

"I've got some good ideas." I stumbled around, grabbing for answers. "Keep in mind, some of the greatest homerun hitters also had records for the most strikeouts. Take Babe Ruth, for example."

"You're not Babe Ruth," Bill said with a smirk. "And in two years, you've yet to deliver a homerun."

"Just a little more time," I begged. *I'm begging? I'm the owner, for crying out loud!* I had to turn this conversation around right now. "I've got a couple of ideas, but I'm still forming them. When I get something solid, I'll let you know, okay? Two months. Give me just two months."

Bill sighed. "Alright, Cleveland. We're all counting on you. I know where you're coming from and I'm trying to get my team to step it up a notch. In fact, our new employee in R&D

is one of the sharpest I've seen in quite some time. I think he's going to come up with something pretty quickly."

"Thanks for reminding me, Bill. I need to get with him soon. I am just swamped for the next few weeks. But after that, he and I will put our heads together and develop something great."

Standing, Bill held out a hand. Shaking mine, he threw out his token phrase. "Now, go out there and win one for the good guys!" I cringe every time I hear that. First of all, he's definitely no Vince Lombardi. Second, this is *not* a game. Third, our competitors are actually the good guys right now.

But what really irritated me about the phrase was that it made me feel like an employee, not the boss. I own the dang company! If I wanted to be treated like an employee, I'd go work for someone else.

"Will do, Bill," I said, shaking his hand heartily. I kept a smile pasted on my face until he left my office.

Boy, was I glad that was done. Now I should have a few weeks to come up with something. Sometimes it really wears me out playing this game with Bill. Although, I have to admit, I'm pretty good at it. Bill always leaves with a smile on his face. When you're a salesman like me, not only can you sell products, you can sell almost anything to anyone. And as long as I could keep Bill somewhat motivated and in place as operations manager, I could still make the money and get to do what I want. Priceless.

Chapter 12

BREAKING BREAD

Now I was faced with the nagging question once again about Camino. Why does this guy want to have lunch with me? Speaking of salesmen, I bet he sells something. Insurance, probably. Those guys are relentless. I bet he saw me in the stands, all alone, and figured me for an easy mark.

I was already in my car, but the thought struck me. *Maybe I shouldn't even show up for lunch.* I don't like being sold to. I like to be the guy doing the pitching, not the catching. I knew *all* of the slick tricks in the book. SPIN Selling, needs analysis, the assumptive close, the trial close, open-ended questions. I knew it all, and I cannot stand it when anybody does it to me.

Then why was my hand turning the key in the ignition? Why was I still heading toward the café? Why was my curiosity getting the better of me?

As I walked into the café, I saw Camino raise his hand and wave. Slightly embarrassed, I looked around. When I realized no one else was watching the exchange, I nodded back at the man as I headed toward the table. Figures he'd get there early. Probably had to scope out the place, seem in control so he could close his deal. Well, we'd see about that.

"Cleve, how's it going?" Camino was standing, pumping my hand before I could even get to the table.

"Ah, good, I guess," I answered. I refused to be an easy mark for this guy. I took the seat across from him and picked up the menu. I knew it like the back of my hand. I brought clients here often. Or rather, I used to. Not a lot of clientele lately, I admitted to myself. Cliff's was a nice restaurant. Not quite white-tablecloth nice, but good food, solid service, and decent prices.

"So, what's good here?" Camino was studying his menu with interest.

I usually get the pulled pork sandwich, but today I was feeling the fish and chips. Of course I wasn't going to give him any extra clues about me. No need to make it easy on the man. I'd pull the salesman card out first and make him order before me. That will help me decide what I'm having. The mirror technique, and I could size him up a little: Steak salad equals a little more highbrow; fish and chips equals simple guy. The waiter came, and we ordered our drinks. Two iced teas, with lemon. He ordered first. I didn't even like iced tea. We went ahead and ordered our meal as well- two steak salads. Mirror technique, baby.

"You think about sales all the time, don't you Cleve?" He was staring at me over his menu, and it was a bit creepy the way he didn't blink as my mouth fell open.

Where did that come from? "Well, sure, I guess," I answered. "I mean, nothing happens until you make a sale, and no sales equals no business. And it is my forte, after all. But I wouldn't say I think about it *all* the time. That would get pretty dull."

"Yes, I'm sure it would," Camino replied, with no conviction in his voice. "So, I bet you want to know what I'm trying to sell to you," Camino started. When my head snapped up, he had one eyebrow raised. "Am I right?"

Dang it, this guy had nailed me! I hate that. "Pretty much, yes," I muttered. I was annoyed now. So much for getting the upper hand. He's clearly a pro. Diffuse the typical and lower the defenses a bit. Here comes the bait.

"Okay, so for starters, I have nothing to sell you, but I can provide you with valuable information," Camino said as the waiter set our teas on the table with a small bowl of lemon wedges.

I started to interject, but he held up one hand for silence while the other squeezed the lemon into his tea. "Don't interrupt." I sat back, chagrined. No one talked to me this way!

"This information will be freely given, and you can decide whether to accept or discard it," he continued. "You don't have to spend a single dime."

"Well, what's the catch?" I couldn't help it, the words were out of my mouth, and now he knew I was hooked. It was like I was helping reel myself in.

"No catch," Camino said. "The only thing I ask in return is your time. The first thing we will do is I will ask you a set of three questions. If you answer them honestly, then we can move forward. If you skirt the truth, I will know and we will be done, and you won't see me again."

Okay, this was definitely a strange selling method, but my fascination was getting the better of me. He said there was no catch, but there *had* to be a catch. There always was. Why did I have to answer questions to hear his spiel? I guess that was part of helping him figure out what to sell to me. He must know I'm competitive. This was a sharp tee-up. Get the guy who likes to be in control think he still is. Most business owners are competitive by nature, and we want what we can't have right up until we get it.

I couldn't help myself. I sipped my super-sweet tea, trying to appear nonchalant, but I knew I was up for the challenge. "Let's do it."

Chapter 13

THE FIRST QUESTION

I saw the transformation myself and still didn't believe it. Camino went from friendly, likable guy, easy going and sort of ho-hum to an eagle-eyed adversary in an instant. His eye color actually seemed to change to a brilliant blue. His intensity was overwhelming as he leaned forward, setting his tea on the table with a tiny snap.

"Are you joyful?" He stared at me, waiting for my answer.

"As in joyful and triumphant? From the Christmas song?" I waited, but he gave no further direction or explanation. "Do you mean am I happy? I mean, of course I am. I have a good job, a pretty wife, nice house, sporty car, two great kids—boy and girl. You know, the perfect family. Of course I'm happy."

The words left my mouth, but I realized they didn't ring true. I *should* be happy. I mean, didn't I have everything? I checked the list again in my mind, and yes, it all added up to happiness. So then why did I feel so uncomfortable with my answer? Why did the words sound so hollow? Maybe I was just imagining it.

"First things first, Cleve," Camino finally broke the silence. "I want to make a distinction between joy and happiness. Happiness is fleeting—it comes and goes. Joy lasts. It's there even when things aren't perfect. Things that are pleasurable make us happy, but even immense pain can't shake true joy. I can see by the look on your face that you don't totally believe me, so let's come back to this one. I want to ask a follow-up question." He put his menu down before leaning forward again.

"Do you look forward to getting up and going to work every morning, and then are you excited when you're on your way home to spend the evening with your family?"

Dang! This guy was nailing me to the wall and it was painful. I was caught. Sheepishly, I tried to formulate a good answer, but all I could manage was, "To be completely honest, my answer would have to be no."

Camino was utterly unfazed. Either that or he was a terrific actor. I saw no indication of surprise in his eyes. "Okay, on to question number two. Do you believe in a higher power?" At my snort, he asked another question. "Do you believe in God?"

Aha! There was the catch! This guy was a Bible beater. He was a fanatic, and he was bent on "converting" me to whatever strange religious thing he was into. Now it all makes sense, and I should've known this was coming. He was here to "save" me.

Well, that was *not* going to happen. Not that I didn't believe there was a higher power. I actually did, but I didn't figure religion was going to help me at all. Religion is the reason for all the wars in the world, and faith is what people use to explain all the things they can't figure out.

It's a nice package to keep the mind from having to think, but science is hot on the trail of faith these days. Besides, some of these religious organizations are so corrupt and have such ridiculous selling schemes they make me look like an angel. I was baptized Catholic, had taken all the typical sacraments, but I'd never really bought into the whole organized religion thing.

There was so much I didn't get, or rather, didn't buy into. But, as it turns out, I do believe in a God. I can't seem to wrap my mind around the earth and all the people on it just being an accident.

I realized Camino was still waiting for my answer. While I'd been lost in my thoughts, the waiter had delivered our steak salads. Giving myself a mental shake, I answered, "I would say yes."

"I mean, I was raised Catholic. Kind of. I don't really go to church anymore though." It actually felt good to get that off my chest, and I didn't know why.

"Okay, last question," Camino said as he drowned his salad in vinaigrette. I couldn't believe he wasn't addressing my answer. Just moving on.

"Do you know God?" My head came up, my fork midway to my mouth. "In other words, do you pray? How would you describe your prayer life? Do you ever set aside time to meditate?"

I was at a loss. Of course I pray. *Please Lord, how about one more big sale this month. Please God, let our pitcher strike this guy out. Please, make it so my kids won't bother me while I watch football tonight.* Somehow I didn't think that was what Camino was talking about.

"I guess I do pray," I admitted.

Camino cocked that eyebrow again, the one that said he didn't really believe me.

"I mean, whenever I really need or want something, I usually ask God for it," I said. It sounded stupid when I said it out loud, but it was actually the honest truth.

"Okay, okay," Camino said as he forked more salad into his mouth. He seemed deep in thought for a moment. Then he snapped back and confidently said, "Let's move forward."

"Wait, what? I passed?" I was full of questions now. "Forward with what?" This was getting weirder and weirder. As quiet as he had been up to this point, Camino's next words took me by surprise.

Chapter 14
THE PITCH

ere's the deal: You're an unhappy man who believes in God, but you have no idea how life really works in order to be truly joyful. Here is my 'pitch.' You knew it was coming in one form or another. I would like to meet with you once a week for the next three weeks." He seemed eager to explain.

"But, I . . ." I trailed off as he continued as if he hadn't heard me.

"I will explain a principle to you and then give you an assignment for the week," Camino said. "Each week we will meet to discuss what you learned from the assignment and then delve into the following week's material. If you are able to "graduate" from the next three weeks' assignments, we shall move on to another series of three lectures and three assignments, if you wish."

I was curious, but this sounded like a lot of work. Assignments? Lectures? I'd already gone to school, thank you very much. Camino forged on.

"What do you say? Are you up for a life-changing challenge?" Camino stared me down, daring me to turn him away.

"This sounds like I'm going back to school," I began slowly. "It doesn't sound like my idea of a good way to pass time. And I'm so busy. I mean, I have clients, and appointments, and stuff, you know . . . ." I trailed off again as I realized he wasn't buying my bull.

That eyebrow was cocked again, and dang it if it didn't make me feel like smacking him in the face. At the same time, I wanted to say yes. Why? Just to prove to him that it wouldn't change anything? Yes, that was probably why. I didn't need this. But, he had nailed me with his little speech about being unhappy and believing in God.

"Let's say for argument's sake that I was up for this little challenge," I started. I saw the light in his eyes, and I knew he was thinking one thing: "I've got this guy on the ropes now. Time to finish the job."

So I forged ahead. "What are you getting out of this? If it's not costing me anything, why do it? Why do you want to 'help' me?" I made crooked air quotes when I said "help" for added emphasis.

"Don't try to change the subject, Cleve," Camino said. "I know you're a man of your word. (How did he know that?) First, a commitment from you, and then I will answer your 'WIIFM' question."

"WIIFM?" Wow. He really is a salesman. Or a good marketer. This was getting deep. "You mean, of course 'What's In It For Me?' Very impressive."

"Exactly," Camino answered patiently. "Now, what's it gonna be?"

I threw the ball back at him. "Well, I want to know more about what I'd have to do. Do I have to take tests or write essays or something?" I absolutely hate school, and it hated me too. If I had to do any "book" work, I was going to tell the guy to take a hike.

"Your assignments will be more of a 'doing' and 'being' nature rather than anything that has to be studied or written," Camino said. "And one field trip. But essentially, it will be you and me talking like we are now, and then you applying the principles to your life. That's it."

Was I actually considering this?

How did I get roped into this? I am still not sure how I qualified for this in the first place. All I did was answer three simple questions. I guess I got them right. Maybe I should have tried to get them wrong? I still had my doubts about what this guy was after. Maybe I shouldn't buy into this deal at all. Just walk away. So what if I wasn't as happy as I could be? I am happy enough. No need to rock the boat.

Chapter 15

THE COMMITMENT

S o, let's move forward," Camino said.

"Okay," I heard someone say. Dang it, it was me! He went for the 'assumptive close' assuming I would immediately follow suit! He got me! How did that just come out of my mouth? I demand a re-answer, like a re-count.

"Great," Camino said with a smile. "To answer your original question. Cleve, this is who I am. It is what I have always done and will always do. I get the satisfaction of seeing real joy in the hearts of people who have begun living the truths I teach."

Whoa. Sounded like a real whack job. And I'd just agreed to follow him? Now I could see how people like that Waco guy had gotten people to blindly throw in and follow them. They were the ultimate salesmen. And here was another one of them. *Tread carefully, Cleve. Don't drink the Kool-Aid.*

His conviction was obvious, and his sincerity rang true. This really was what he lived for, but that didn't make it true. That didn't make it right for me. But, when I took a good, hard look at my life, I realized I was definitely missing something. My business was failing. Honestly, it was in the toilet, and it just hadn't circled the bowl for the final time yet. My family life was lame, to say the least. Cindy and I hadn't had a romantic evening in longer than I cared to admit, and the last time I did anything real with either of my kids was years ago.

So, what could it hurt? If it didn't work, I probably wouldn't be any worse off than I was now. But what if it did work? Camino was genuine. He was one of the most "real" people I had come across in quite some time. Small talk was over. His demeanor changed and I realized the buildup was over. He'd made the sale. Now it was time to get down to brass tacks.

Camino launched into relating the key concepts that would set the tone for our future times together. "The unexamined life is not worth living." I looked at him. He looked at me. "Socrates. Many people have heard this phrase before, but a lot of people haven't heard what Aristotle said later."

Was I waiting on bated breath? Yes, I was actually on the edge of my seat, my salad forgotten. Camino paused and then continued.

"The unplanned life is not worth examining." He smiled at me. "That was Aristotle."

"Is this going to be a philosophy lesson?" I joked. One look from Camino had me buttoning my lip, so to speak.

"We have to take a hard look at ourselves on a regular basis and then plan our future. Otherwise someone else will plan it for us," Camino said seriously. "So, Cleve, the first thing we have to do is cover a few basics. Then we can jump into our first topic."

Eagerly, I waited for him to move on. I didn't know if the pauses were for dramatic effect or not, but they were working. I was dying to know what came next.

Chapter 16

THE BASICS

irst, what is a human being?" Camino paused again.

I had no idea if the question was a rhetorical one or if he wanted an actual answer. That was a pretty stupid question. Why does it matter? He didn't give me more time to answer. Instead, he forged ahead.

"One of the best definitions is this: the human person is a rational being made up of a body and spirit created to be happy," Camino said. "So, this leads to the question of what can humans do in simple terms to be happy?"

Again, I was thinking this was a rhetorical question, but the silence lasted long enough to prompt me to answer. "I don't know what you're looking for, Camino," I began. "I mean, are you asking what can we do—physically? Like eating and sleeping?"

"Well, I guess technically you're on the right track, but I was going in a different direction," Camino said with a slight smile. "We have intellect—thinking, we have passions and emotions—feeling, and we have actions and free will—doing."

I could agree with that. I nodded, silently urging him to get to the point.

"One of the greatest challenges of today's society is how much emphasis is placed on feelings," he continued. "Even some so-called life experts espouse a greater focus on feelings is necessary. But in actuality, feelings are fleeting."

He had me thinking. My feelings lately were certainly all over the map. I went from giddiness when I was almost bombed from a night at Ted's to anger when I got home and received the third degree from Cindy for being late, to a swagger of confidence when I continued to hold Bill off from jumping ship. None of those feelings lasted very long, however. Camino was still talking, and I was missing it.

". . . instinctive too, and many times, our instincts, such as hunger and anger, for example, can lead us away from what is ultimately good for us." He must have sensed my hackles rising, because he put his hands up in the familiar "hold on" gesture. "Don't get me wrong, Cleve, they're still important. When directed appropriately, they can be very good. But they aren't as important as the other two things humans can do. You see, thoughts and actions are far more important, but here's the rub," Camino said after another of his brief pauses. "We simply don't set aside time to think." He waited, whether for a response or effect, I don't know, but now I was getting annoyed.

Chapter 17

THINK TIME

"T ime to think?" I leaned forward. "Who has time to think? In my business, you have to stay one step ahead of everyone else, and you have to react based on instincts and knowledge as well as experience. And what am I supposed to be thinking about? That's time I can spend with my kids, my wife, whatever."

"Or at the game, or at a bar unwinding?" He had me there. Okay, so maybe I had some extra time where I could be thinking, but I needed that time to relax, unwind, and just *be*.

"We rarely make time to pause over the noise, especially given today's world with all its technologies," Camino continued, glancing at my ever-present smartphone. "And so, our actions are often the by-product of feelings created from some marketing campaign or because the people around us suggest we act in a certain way."

So I guess I could agree with that one, since I was rarely more than two feet from my phone, and if I came into the office and people were in a panic, it automatically set my mind racing too. I waited.

"So, we just go along," he said. "Yet, if we had thought through it a little more or even walked away and paused for some 'thinking' time first, we may have taken a different action. Do you agree?"

"Yeah, I sometimes do rush into things without thinking, but for the most part that makes me better," I pushed back. "A better businessman, a better husband, a better father."

"Really? Think back to your last exchange with your wife," Camino said. "Was there anything you said that you wish you could've taken back as soon as you said it?"

I'm sure he could see it written across my face, but I hurried to compose my expression. I knew I'd put my foot in my mouth with Cindy last night when she talked about me never changing. I knew it as soon as the words were out of my mouth. How did Camino know?

"Well, I mean, yeah, sure, there's always something you wish you could say differently," I started. "I'm not going to win the Husband of the Year award." I chuckled, but Camino's stare cut me down.

"Okay, what about your kids?"

"My kids? What about them?" My back was up again. I was a decent father. I mean, I thought so anyway.

"How is your relationship with them? Do you think it could be better?" Camino waited again.

"Sure, sure," I said quickly. "It could always be better, right? But I'm a pretty good father. They get everything they need and most of the stuff they want."

"That's not what I'm talking about, Cleve, and you know it," Camino said patiently. "But let's move on, because I think I've proven my point." I started to object, but he just rolled over my reaction.

"So, one of our goals over the next few weeks is to prioritize your thinking," he said. "And ultimately, this gets back to examining and planning. These are critical activities to ensure we are living meaningful, joyful lives. Make sense so far?"

Well, sure, it made sense, but that didn't mean I was completely on board yet. "Well, I never took a class in philosophy or theology so I don't know how much deeper you're going to go, but so far so good," I said smartly. "I mean, I understand it, but of course, I'm a bit skeptical. I probably think a little more than the average person."

Camino tipped his head, urging me to continue.

"I'm not the best planner," I admitted. "I tend to get caught up in the day-to-day activities too much. But honestly, Camino, all this talk these days about strategic planning is for guys who have too much time on their hands. At the end of the day, we can't predict the future anyway, so why spend a bunch of time thinking about it?"

"I understand your position, Cleve," Camino responded.

Boy, I just couldn't ruffle this guy's feathers! He was cool as a cucumber, and I found myself envious of his peaceful demeanor. I was hurling veiled insults at him and he was just as calm as when he'd ordered his meal.

"There are steps that need to be taken in a company before authentic planning can take place," Camino continued. "This is definitely something we can cover down the road, but first we need to lay the foundation and overcome your natural skepticism on where joy comes from."

Well, who wouldn't want to be more joyful? I figured it couldn't hurt to hear him out, but I was still not a believer.

"Let's get started," Camino said.

Started? I thought we'd already started. My lunch hour was going to be over soon. Ha. My assistant knew I took long lunches, so she wasn't expecting me back, but Camino didn't have to know that. I checked my watch pointedly.

"You've got time, Cleve," Camino said with a knowing smile. When I stared at him, the disbelief must've been evident on my face. I sat back, prepared to take whatever he was going to dish out.

Chapter 18

TRUTH

T he first topic is Truth, with a capital T," Camino said simply. "Unfortunately, in today's society, we have lost our sense of the fullness of Truth. We are so caught up in compromise and ultimately in human respect that the clear blue sky of Truth has become the gray storm clouds of confusion."

Okay, I was with him so far. The line was getting blurred. I nodded, encouraging him to continue.

"The priority of divine respect has become, at best, an afterthought and at worst, completely eliminated from any meaningful consideration. So, we need to begin with Truth," Camino added. "And since I realize this is going to be a tough sell for you, I thought I would throw you an underhand pitch, to give you a better chance at knocking it out of the park."

Dang, he was using baseball analogies now. My weakness, and my personal favorite, in the selling game. I had to confess, the guy had a way with words. Direct, matter-of-fact delivery, but his words had a sincere passion behind them. I could literally feel every word he spoke. Of course, I would never admit to him that I could sense it.

"I get where you're going with this," I said. "I mean, it seems like we're all trying so hard to get along that we've lost the basis for how to get along in the first place."

"Exactly!" Camino's expression held a true grin now as if he felt like he was really making headway with me. "Technology is a great thing, but it's brought the distant closer together and the proximate farther apart. On the good side, it's made our world smaller by providing a greater potential for more connections. But on the flip side, a neighbor is more likely to ask to borrow a tool via text or e-mail than to just come over and knock on your door. So we leave it on our porch so he can pick it up and have him drop it back off on the porch when he's done."

"The sad thing about that is I know you're right, because I've done it," I agreed sheepishly. "I just never stepped back to assess whether it's good or bad." I could admit to myself, if not Camino just yet, that I was becoming increasingly interested in where this conversation was going.

"Okay, so I sense the homework portion of this session coming up," I said dryly. "Lay it on me, Camino." I attempted to feign a look of disinterest, but in reality, I was kind of looking forward to what he had to say. Maybe he had a magic recipe for success, happiness, and this elusive joy he kept talking about.

"We cannot speak of Truth without speaking of God, but since you've already said you believe in God, we don't have to delve super deep," Camino said.

"There are great resources that prove God exists through reason alone," Camino went on. "The most obvious is how the world began. The big bang theory could've happened, but where did the matter come from that exploded in the first place? There has to be a first cause. Everything comes from somewhere. And therefore, everything has to lead back to something or someone. And we call this person God."

He paused to take a sip of tea. I did the same, barely managing to keep the look of disgust off my face. "Cleve, why don't you just ask her for a glass of ice water?"

I froze, my hand in midair before I set the glass back down. This man was good. I'd carefully schooled my features to mask my distaste, but he'd still picked up on it. Mirror technique foiled. Sheesh this guy was too much. "That obvious, huh?" I chuckled.

"No, actually it's not, but I've become somewhat of an expert at reading people," Camino shrugged and then lifted a finger. "My friend here would like a glass of water." The server nodded as she backed away from the table with our empty plates.

"Okay, so back to our discussion," Camino said. "Even if you don't believe this or any other rational argument, just consider Pascal's Wager."

Again, I was lost. I wasn't familiar with all the jargon he was throwing at me, but I remained fairly interested anyway.

"Just in case you're not familiar with it, let me expand on it," Camino said. "If you act on earth like there is no God and find out there is, you're likely going to deeply regret the way you acted. But if you act on earth like there is a God and find out later there isn't one, what have you lost? So we might as well all act as if there is a God and cover ourselves just in case. You've already told me you believe in God, so I don't think I need to go much farther, do I?"

I shook my head, but in reality, my mind was reeling. I'd never heard it put quite that way before, but I didn't know how to respond without sounding uneducated. Oh well, he somehow seems to know me pretty well already anyway, so maybe I should just admit it.

"Okay, so I've never heard someone explain it like that before," I said. "It makes sense." And it really did the more I thought about it.

"Keep in mind, though, that while faith isn't needed until further down the road, it is still necessary to get us all the way home," Camino continued with a clear tone of caution.

Chapter 19

SCIENCE

A lright, we're going to continue our discussion with some of the conclusions from the positive psychology movement," Camino said.

Oh boy, here it comes. What *it* was, I had no idea, but I felt like the hammer was about to drop. "So?" That came out wrong, but I really just wanted Camino to get to the point.

"There is an astonishing convergence across the millennia, spanning geography and culture with respect to the concept of virtue or, in other terms, principles to live by."

Camino went on. "There are six primary guiding principles inherent to virtually all cultures throughout time: self-esteem, good looks, assertiveness, autonomy, uniqueness, and wealth."

Now I really *was* confused. Camino must have sensed it, because he laughed. "Okay, just kidding," he said. "Those are the virtues we see in many areas of today's society, unfortunately. Actually, wisdom, courage, love, justice, temperance and transcendence are the universal virtues as evidenced by modern research, more specifically within the science of positive psychology."

"Okay, most of those make sense to me," I answered. "Being smart and gutsy and fair seem pretty obvious. But I'm not really sure what transcendence is." Inwardly, I was wincing. This seemed to be going spiritual and outside my comfort zone.

"Essentially, transcendence means the acknowledgement of a higher power; a belief in God," Camino said. "This is prevalent across all cultures of all time. Here's an interesting point. As you are Catholic, you should appreciate this: Thomas Aquinas' list of virtues is as close to this final list as anyone else's. As you probably know, Aquinas lived eight hundred years ago and yet these core virtues are as applicable to us today as they were in his time."

My memory was foggy, but I remembered something about a guy named Aquinas from my childhood catechism classes. I tried to focus on what Camino was saying now.

"Incidentally, more has been written and studied about Aquinas than any other philosopher or theologian who has ever lived," he continued. "His list of virtues is as follows: faith, hope, charity, prudence, justice, fortitude, and temperance. He called the first three the theological virtues and the last four the cardinal virtues. But really, these are in essence an expansion on earlier virtues developed by Aristotle."

Okay, now I was really lost. Sure, some of those sounded familiar, but I was struggling to understand why we were talking about them at this point.

"Do you remember why he called the last four the cardinal virtues?" Camino was staring at me now.

"Nope," I admitted simply. "I think it was something about them being the most important, but I really couldn't say for sure."

"Well, you're not far from the truth," Camino said brightly. "Cardinal means 'hinge.' Aquinas believed all other virtues hinged on those four. Let's take the first list from modern science and compare it to Aquinas' list." He was drawing on a napkin now. I had no idea where the pen had come from, but he was scribbling away. He grabbed my napkin to complete the picture.

Transcendence = Faith, Hope

Love= Charity

Wisdom= Prudence

Justice= Justice

Courage= Fortitude

Temperance= Temperance

"The lists are pretty much exact, wouldn't you agree?" I had to admit, I did agree. He had turned the napkins so I was able to read them easily.

"I really like Ben Franklin's thirteen virtues too, which can all be traced back to this list as well," Camino said. "These are truly 'universal' principles."

It *was* pretty interesting, when I stopped to think about it. How did a guy eight hundred years ago figure out a list of principles that today we can safely say are still considered universal? I still had some reservations though.

"So what if we know these things?" I was playing Mr. Cool again. "What difference does it make and what does it mean? I'm a nuts-and-bolts guy when it comes to information. I mean, this touchy-feely stuff does nothing for me."

"I understand," Camino said, smiling that mysterious smile again. "Would it be fair to say that someone espousing all these virtues is living a 'good' life?"

I was squirming on the inside. This was where he was going to nail me to the wall yet again. I gave a typical noncommittal shrug.

Chapter 20

VIRTUE OVERVIEW

Aristotle said that a good life is one built on virtue," he went on. "Without virtue, one can not be happy. To him, authentic happiness was rooted in doing good and avoiding evil. This is one of the best and first steps toward living a joyful life. The big question to you is this: Do you, Cleve Gordon, embrace all of these virtues?"

This was where the rubber met the road. No one could possibly be that good, so how could I say yes? But to say no was admitting my flaws. So I went with the best compromise.

"Well, considering this is the first I have been exposed to this thinking, I'm not sure what I would say to answer that question," I said. "Are there some principles that are more important than others?" Now I was stalling.

"Yes, in a sense there are," Camino answered. "Let's picture the virtues as a tree. The support structures would be the theological virtues, with faith as the roots, then hope and charity as the trunk of the tree. The branches could be considered the four cardinal virtues and the leaves of the tree could be the other human virtues like cheerfulness, humility, and so forth."

"Okay, I'm with you so far," I said, encouraging him to continue. I wasn't looking at my watch anymore. I was on my way to being fascinated by the conversation.

"The key is to water the tree so faith may grow and give the tree enough light, or Truth (with a capital T), so the virtues can blossom. So, let's take a quick look at those virtues. There are a lot of great resources I could share with you that go into much greater detail if you are interested later, but for now I will simply provide an overview."

"Faith is essentially the belief in God and that He is ultimately in control," Camino began. "Hope is believing that this life is not all there is. For example, we are hopeful that when we die, there is a place (which most people call heaven) where we can go and be eternally happy with our God. Charity is essentially the love for God and other people for the sake of God. These are the theological virtues, and the ones that come directly from God."

"Makes sense," I said. "So then the cardinal virtues are next?"

"Exactly," Camino said with a smile. "Now you're getting it. They are more or less acquired. Prudence is wisdom, which is knowing right from wrong. Justice is giving God what is due to him and then giving others what is right as well. Fortitude is the courage to 'stay on track,' or constantly strive toward the good. Temperance is about moderation and balance. The realization that too much of a good thing is actually not always a good thing."

"Whew! That's a lot to take in," I admitted. My head was starting to feel very full.

"Do you have any questions so far?" Camino was sitting back, his hands steepled together on the table in front of him.

"This all sounds great, but I still don't understand how these virtues are supposed to make me happy?" I needed some time to process this information, but I knew Camino had more to say.

"Without virtue, we cannot live an authentically good life, which to most means a life of happiness," Camino said. "Therefore, without an understanding of virtue, we cannot know what an authentically good and happy life is. Make sense?"

"Ah, yeah, that makes sense, I guess."

"Cleve, when are you going to get to the point where you don't feel like you have to impress me with your skills of evasion?"

The question stopped me. I mean, I wasn't evading him, not really. Was I? Before I could stumble into an answer, Camino continued.

"We can't hit a target if we have nothing to aim at," he said. "We can't achieve what we can't conceive. Truth is knowledge.

It begins with humility. Truth is achieved through a quest for knowledge, and virtue is knowledge acted upon with humility. "

He wasn't giving me time to breathe between the shots now. Left hook, right hook; I was on the ropes. Yes, now I was into boxing terms, but it was how I felt. The life I thought- or better yet, pretended- was so wonderful seemed to be crumbling around me as Camino continued to share his words with me.

"Something we'll come back to is fortitude, and along with that, magnanimity," Camino said. "This is striving toward greatness and believing we can achieve wonderful things on this earth with the talents we've been given. But again, humility must come right along with it or we could be headed for trouble. It's very easy to allow our pride to get the best of us, and to think we alone control everything and we alone deserve the credit."

I was reeling. I was trying to pay attention to what he was saying, but I was still seeing the remnants of the so-called "perfect life" I'd thought I had burning all around me.

"Cleve?" My eyes focused, and I realized Camino had been staring at me. How long he'd been just sitting there silently, I had no idea. I'd just had a moment. My perfect life wasn't perfect at all, and it had taken a perfect stranger to point it out.

"We're going to drill down to the most important practical virtue now, okay?" Camino waited for my nod, then stopped me in my tracks again with his next question.

Chapter 21

GUT CHECK

C leve, do you love your wife?" Surely this was a trick question. Of course I loved my wife. Why would I have married her if I didn't love her? I answered him as truthfully as I knew how.

"Yes, of course I love her."

"How?"

"How?" I was confused. "What do you mean how?"

"I mean, if she were here and I asked her how she knows you love her, what would she say?" Camino waited.

My heart was pounding. Of course Cindy knew I loved her, right? My mind raced to find a way she would know that I could express to Camino. "Well, I think she would say she knows I love her because I provide for the family and take care of things around the house," I said.

Camino's head tilted and I rushed on. "I'm pretty good at remembering her birthday and our anniversary. I usually get her flowers when I screw up, and I tell her I love her. I'm sure she could come up with some other things too."

Dead silence. What was Camino thinking? Were those crickets chirping? I was pretty sure by the look on his face that I had failed this part of the discussion. But really, what kind of question was it anyway? Love is unexplainable. I know there is the whole "in love" versus "choosing to love" debate, but at the end of the day, it's not that big of a deal.

Camino was still staring at me, his lips pursed in concentration. Wow. I must've really blown it. But basically, you find the right woman, marry her, take the vows and stuff, and then things are super hot and fun for about the first six months and then reality sets in. The passion dulls as the reality of work and bills, mortgages and insurance, in-laws and kids and pets sets in. Hmm . . . maybe that's all there was. Now I was starting to depress myself, and Camino was *still* just staring at me. It was getting pretty awkward. I sipped my water, grateful I was no longer drinking the sweet tea.

Chapter 22

ASSIGNMENT #1

Finally, Camino leaned forward. "Okay, Cleve, here's your first assignment," he said ominously.

Oh boy. Now I was getting worried. What had I said that had led him to this assignment, and what was he going to ask me to do? Was I going to have to take Cindy out on a fancy date? Wine, roses, the whole nine yards? I mean, I could do that. Sure, it'd been a while since we'd done something like that. Probably five or six years, but I could do it. The last time we'd gone out, it had been so awkward. She'd been angry about something I'd done and we'd left the restaurant before dessert. I realized Camino was waiting for my attention.

"Alright, man, lay it on me," I said confidently.

"I want you to demonstrate you love your wife on a daily basis without her figuring out that you are doing anything out of the ordinary," Camino said. "Don't get me wrong; she should notice, but she should have difficulty putting her finger on it."

Show her I love her without her realizing it? Now I really *was* confused. I felt my hackles rise. "How the heck am I supposed to do that? And why should I do more than what I'm already doing? I work hard. Real hard. I have stresses that you wouldn't believe if I told you! I do more than most husbands do as it is. Cindy doesn't have to nag me to get the yard work done or get the cars serviced. I'm not sure how I could do any more even if I wanted to."

"Then how is it that you have time to go to baseball games?" Camino's question caught me off guard. Ouch.

"Listen, you're a nice guy, so I'm not going to say what I really want to say right now," I started out sarcastically. "I need baseball to relieve stress."

"And stops at the bar too?" Camino smiled knowingly.

"Hey, I don't need you judging me," I shot back. "Do you know what it's like to be a high-powered business owner? It ain't easy, that's for sure. I work hard all day and then I need to play hard to make things even out. If I didn't have those releases I have now, I'm not sure I could even stay married, let alone be the solid husband and father I am today."

"Look, Cleve, I understand your stress. I do. But I'm not suggesting a vacation to Maui. Do you have time to write her a quick encouraging note? What about calling her out of the blue in the middle of the day to tell her you appreciate her? Unload the dishwasher? Make the bed before she does? Spend five minutes listening to her tell about her day without interrupting her? Do a load of laundry? Have coffee together?"

"Wow, Camino, I'm tired already," I said. "Nice list. Your wife must be real lucky."

"I've never been married." What? This guy was trying to give me marital advice and he'd never been married?

"Hold on a minute," I protested. "You've never—"

"We're not talking about me," Camino interrupted. "Just answer my question, Cleve."

"Fine. I'm sure I have some time to do some of those things, but Cindy and I have things worked out as far as who has what responsibility," I said. "I do outside work; she does inside work. This keeps it even as far as workloads around the house."

Chapter 23

TIP THE SCALES

T hen make it uneven." I'm sure my jaw had dropped at the suggestion, but I would never forget his point. It hit me like a ton of bricks. Surely I could manage to unload the dishwasher once a week. That would shock the heck out of her!

"Okay, I think I get it," I said slowly.

"I can see that you do," Camino agreed. "Tip the scales in her favor. Help out more than you normally would. Come home earlier. Give up things you like to do in order to do more things she would like to do. This is true charity. *This* is love. Losing oneself in order to go beyond the needs and desires of another. Do this and your marriage will grow stronger than you ever imagined."

I still wasn't sure about coming home early. I really needed Ted's. But I would love to see her jaw drop when she opened the dishwasher and found it empty! Ha! Or maybe I'll bring her flowers tonight for no reason. My mind was racing again. This felt somewhere between a punch in the jaw and a divine revelation.

Even though I was embarrassed to hear about all the little ways I could've been loving my wife over the years, I still understood what he was saying. What he said was pure truth. And hard as heck to swallow at the same time. I realized he was staring at me again.

"Okay," I said sheepishly.

"Okay?" Camino tilted his head again.

"I mean, okay, I'm in," I said, firmly now.

"Great," Camino said. "Let's meet again, same time, same place in one week. I'm looking forward to hearing about your experiences." Then he just walked out, leaving me with the bill.

Of course. I might've been mad if I hadn't felt like laughing. I shook my head, threw a couple twenties on the table and headed back to work.

I'd like to say I became the ultimate husband overnight. I'd like to say my wife now runs to the door to smother me with kisses when I get home before presenting me with a four-course meal she made just for me. I'd like to say it, but I can't. Because I sucked at homework.

Chapter 24

HOME PART DEUX

oney, I'm home!" I barreled through the door from the garage into our kitchen. I could smell something spicy cooking. Cindy's homemade spaghetti sauce. I'd bet anything on it.

"Cleve?" Cindy rounded the corner into the kitchen. "Are you sick?" Cautiously, she approached me. The shock was evident when I shoved the roses into her arms.

"Red's your favorite, right?" I grinned. "And no, I'm not sick. I just thought I'd come home early."

"Well, uh, actually no, I prefer yellow, but that's okay, I mean, what's going on?" Cindy's skepticism was obvious.

I couldn't get everything right the first time. *Yellow. Gotta remember that.* She laid the flowers on the counter but before she could reach for her favorite vase, I plucked it from the top of the cabinet. Handing it to her, I saw the surprise register before pleasure bloomed. She looked away, blushing. *Whoa! Might just be something to all this!*

"Alright, Cleveland," Cindy said, putting her hands on her hips as the vase filled with water. "Out with it. Did you lose your job? Stupid question—you can't lose your job." She threw up one hand to stop me from answering as she shut the water off and started putting flowers into the vase.

"Are you and the guys planning another weeklong golf trip?"

"No, it's nothing at all," I started. "I just realized I have been a bit selfish lately and wanted to show you I love you and that I want to be a better husband." Okay, so I blew the "don't let her know what's going on" part of Camino's assignment, but I was so excited with the results I'd gotten in the first two minutes of the experiment, I couldn't help it!

Clearly I really have been a bit of a jerk if this is the reaction I get when I do something nice for her. To be honest, I typically take two guys-only trips a year. One to fish and one to golf. And sometimes I throw in a Vegas weekend or two. I guess I usually try buttering her up to get less flack for leaving the family when I come home with one of those plans.

"How are the kids?"

She almost dropped the vase, but I reached out to steady it before she met my eyes.

"Jenna's fine as always. Go see for yourself with Brian," she said. "He's in his room." *Laying it on a little too thick, buddy. She still thinks you're up to something.*

Chapter 25

FATHER-SON TIME

K nock, knock?" I peered into Brian's room. He looked up from where he was doing his homework on his bed.

"Dad, I'm doing the best I can in math, okay? Can you just leave me alone for once?" He dismissed me.

"Look, Brian, I have something I need to tell you," I said. "I would appreciate just a few minutes of your time, and no, it's not a lecture."

He rolled his eyes, but he sat up, crossing his arms over his chest. "Fine." I could tell by his deep sigh that he still thought he was going to get an earful from me. I guess that was fair, since I couldn't remember the last time I'd come into his room for any other reason than to talk to him about something negative.

"Okay, so you know how I stretched the truth on the phone when we were in the car?"

"You mean when you lied to Bill?" Ouch. Brian was drilling me with his eyes now, daring me to deny it.

"Uh, yeah, okay, I did lie, and it was wrong," I began. I thought his eyes were going to bug out of his head, but his defensive posture relaxed a bit. "You were right. I didn't set a good example for you then, and I'm not sure I've been setting a good one for you at all. I just want you to know that I'm going to try to do better. And so, um, what I wanted to say is . . ." I trailed off. I had a knot in my throat. This was harder than I thought.

"What? Dad, what did you want to say?" Brian was curious now.

I swallowed, trying to get rid of the lump, but decided I'd just have to say the words quickly. Rip off the bandage. "I'm sorry, Brian."

Brian's face paled slightly and it was a moment before he spoke. "Wow. I, uh, don't know what to say." Another moment of silence and then he stood, holding out his hand.

"I guess, thanks?" He wanted to shake my hand. I took it and shook it once, firmly.

"You're welcome, Son," I said. I probably should've hugged him, but I hadn't made it quite that far in my transition, and at this point, my apology almost sent my son into a coma, so a hug might just push him over the edge. Leaving the room, I let out a big sigh. That was harder than I had thought it would be, but it felt right.

Chapter 26
SLOW START

So again, the evening was a bit strange. Jenna just kept to herself in blissful ignorance of the issues going on in our family. Her time would come to contribute. Unfortunately. Cindy and Brian both snuck glances at me during dinner. I pretended not to notice, but when their jaws dropped as I rinsed my plate and put it in the dishwasher, I barely held back a laugh.

Things were pretty normal the rest of the evening, so when I woke up today I thought things would be good. When I decided to go into the office for a few hours, Cindy let me know what she thought.

"Cleve, you can't come home half an hour early one night, bring me flowers, and think everything's fine," she snapped. "You were pretty pleased with yourself last night, but then today you're back to the office on a Saturday. Great. Go have a good time."

She slammed the door to our room as I looked back at Brian. "It'll only be a few hours, okay? We'll shoot some hoops when I get back."

"Sure, Dad," Brian answered, but the disbelief was evident in his voice.

What didn't they get about this? I was a changed man, couldn't they tell that? I couldn't spend all my spare time with them. This was a work in progress. So why was I sitting in my office thinking about them instead of doing the paperwork I came to do?

"It's all Camino's fault," I said to no one. My voice echoed in the empty room. What had this guy gotten me into? I do one nice thing and then they expect me to just completely change and they get mad when I inform them I will still be going to the office for a while on Saturdays? I was starting to think my efforts had been completely worthless.

Sunday was pretty normal, with Cindy and the kids going to church while I slept in. Then I watched baseball all afternoon as Cindy played a board game with the kids. On Monday, I made an effort to get home early again, stopping for only two drinks at Ted's. Again, Cindy expressed surprise, but her smile was a bit forced when I handed her the yellow roses.

She'd thanked me for the flowers, even going so far as to pat me on the shoulder, but it didn't seem sincere. The week flew by, and to be completely honest, I didn't really try very hard to ace my homework. Tuesday I stopped at the bar as usual and Thursday I watched a ball game at a buddy's house and came home late. But the key was, I did feel different for some reason. Something had changed. At least a little.

Chapter 27

CAMINO, PART TWO

S o, how did it go?" Camino didn't waste any time. As soon as the server took our order and walked away, he got right down to it.

"Well, other than letting the cat out of the bag a bit early, I think it went fairly well," I answered. "I think I confused Cindy pretty good. And I do feel a little bit better about myself." That part was completely true. I didn't know how to explain it, but once when I was a kid, I sort of ended up helping a friend of mine without expecting anything in return. The feeling I had after that incident was how I was feeling now when Cindy would look at me strangely after doing the dishes or bringing her flowers.

"Okay, good, I'm glad to hear that, Cleve," Camino said with a grin. "It might take Cindy a while to embrace the 'new' you, but she will. You might notice she will have a natural tendency to be a bit nicer to you as well. But this isn't always the case. Just stick to the plan because the love you're demonstrating is like the rainfall a budding flower needs to blossom."

"Yeah, I can totally understand that—I mean, just this morning she actually kissed me on the cheek on the way out the door!" I was grinning like a schoolboy. "That hasn't happened in, um . . . well, let's just say it's been way too long."

"That's the wonderful thing about love, Cleve," Camino responded. "The more you give, the more you want to give and the less the immediate results matter, because authentic love is inherently unselfish yet unquestionably life changing for the person who gives it as well as the person who receives it. We will see this specifically in action on our field trip. But first, let's recap what you've learned so far."

Chapter 28

RECAP

He leaned forward as the server moved back after delivering our sandwiches. "There is Truth, and you made at least some strides to see this, right?"

I nodded, but I had to tell him about my experience with Brian. "I apologized to my son for not being a good example to him in the car the other day, and I thought he was going to drop dead," I said with a chuckle. "It's not funny, I realize that, but it sure did feel good afterwards. It wasn't easy."

"It never is, but it does get easier," Camino said. "That's a great step toward Truth. I'm sure you would agree there are universal principles and that these include what can also be termed virtues."

At my nod, he continued. "The greatest is love, with charity as its highest form," he recapped. "This is why you were able to make some fast changes—because you implemented specific actions to demonstrate this to your family. There is hardly anything more powerful. Keep it up."

"Keep it up?" I knew he was going to say it, but it still seemed impossible. "I'm just starting to realize I haven't been as good as I thought for a long time, so I'm not sure I can keep it up."

"Forget yourself," Camino replied. "Put your wants and needs second to theirs. Continue to develop your relationship with your family based on finding out more about their desires while keeping yours in check. You saw results fairly early, but they will cease to continue unless you continue the practice you've begun. Now, let's get out of here. Today's our field day, and I call this week Life, with a capital L."

Camino was ignoring the fact that I'd only taken a few bites from my sandwich, and he hadn't even touched his, yet I still had to throw another twenty on the table on the way out. What was going on, and what was so important that we couldn't finish our meal first?

Chapter 29

LITTLE SISTERS

As we were riding in the car, our conversation drifted to small talk. I could tell he wanted to keep our destination a surprise, so I didn't mention it. I noticed we were getting closer and closer to the bad part of town. My stomach sank when he turned into a neighborhood I usually try to avoid at all costs. When we pulled into one of the driveways, I barely contained my groan.

"We're here!" He seemed excited. I expected to start dodging bullets any moment. He got out without locking his car. Seriously? His car was no prize, but still, it had four wheels and could certainly be fun for some passersby to take for a joyride. Why make it easier?

We went up to the door, but before Camino could knock, the door opened and there stood a nun in her typical gray suit. A habit, that's what they were called. I only remembered that because I always thought they looked like something I could never get in the "habit" of wearing. I actually didn't think they wore those things anymore.

I kept my joke to myself as we were welcomed inside the humble structure. "Welcome," said the nun. "I'm Sister Marguerite." I didn't think that was her real name, because I was pretty sure I remembered they had to use a different name when they became a nun, or something like that. Later, I found out from Camino that her real name was Theresa Novak, and she had indeed changed her name when she took her vows. She'd chosen the name Marguerite because of the woman's enduring faith as a missionary.

The woman seemed very calm. Like she was at peace with herself. I don't know why that dawned on me. Probably because I don't think I'd ever felt like that. Interesting. "Sister Marguerite, I'd like to introduce you to my friend Cleveland Gordon," Camino said. "He's going to be joining us today."

She took my hand in both of hers, and again I was struck by her calm demeanor. She didn't seem to be in a hurry at all. I, on the other hand, was always rushing somewhere. Except when I was at Ted's. Or in my chair at home, watching a game with a beer in my hand.

I was drawn back into the conversation when Camino asked, "So, is everyone ready?"

"Yes, Camino," she replied. "We are ready."

Chapter 30

DISCOMFORT ZONE

We turned and left through the door we'd just entered. Camino and I followed behind Sister Marguerite, and Camino gave me a brief synopsis of what we were getting into. "She is part of a community called the Little Sisters of the Lamb," he whispered. "They were founded in France, and part of their normal course of action was to beg for food."

At my look, he smiled. "I know it sounds strange, but this is what they still do today," Camino said. "They don't keep food on hand, and they go door-to-door asking for food every single night. They typically live in one of the worst neighborhoods in a city and believe God will protect them and provide for them."

I was shocked, and quite nervous about knocking on any doors in this neighborhood. Quietly, I voiced my concerns. "Are we seriously going to knock on doors with her? Aren't these people poor? Or drug dealers? I mean, aren't they people who either wouldn't or couldn't share food with total strangers?"

"It's going to be okay, Cleve," Camino reassured me. "You need to see this."

No, I don't, was what I wanted to say, but in the end, I kept my mouth shut. We walked three blocks before we knocked on the first door. I was hoping I would've calmed down a bit, but if anything, I was more nervous than before. I realized we were a pretty odd group. Two guys in business casual attire and three nuns in their habits. Maybe no one would answer the door.

I tensed up when I heard the locks click and the door creak open. Behind the door was a sweet-looking elderly woman. She was wearing a flower print housecoat, and her hair was covered in plastic. Her dark skin sagged around her face and neck, but her smile was what really caught my eye. I tried not to stare as I realized she was missing most of her front teeth.

"How can I help you?" She leaned heavily on the door.

Chapter 31

DON'T JUDGE A BOOK BY ITS COVER

W e are Sisters of the Little Lamb," Sister Marguerite responded. "Might you have some bread to spare? We have nothing to eat."

I was feeling pretty ridiculous. I'd just had some bread. On a plate. With tomatoes, bacon, and cheese, and I'd paid for it and left it sitting there. I could've brought it for the Little Lambs, or whatever they were called. I was as nervous as I'd been on my first sales call. My palms were sweaty, and I felt if I opened my mouth, the words would come tumbling out in a rush.

Thankfully, the Sisters seemed to be doing all the talking. Suddenly, I realized the door was opened wider and the nuns were heading in the house. What? "Bless you," Sister Marguerite said, touching the woman's shoulder as she entered the small home. Camino gestured to me, indicating I should go first, so I swallowed hard and stepped inside.

"I might have a little something for you all," the woman said as she made her way past us and into the kitchen. All I could think about was how wrong this all seemed. She couldn't have much at all, looking at her tattered furniture and paint peeling from the walls. Why in the world was a successful guy like me standing here asking her to give *me* something? And why would she be willing to give us anything?

We found ourselves crowded around her kitchen table as Esther, as she'd introduced herself, prepared food for us to eat. To say the next thirty minutes were surreal would be an understatement. Despite the peeling paint and the state of her furniture, Esther's house was immaculate, and it was obvious she took pride in her home. Actually, I hate to admit it, but it might've been a little neater than my own house.

Before we knew it, she was passing around mashed potatoes and a delicious gravy, along with bread she'd obviously made herself. The bread melted in my mouth and I forked away the potatoes and gravy while conversation took place around me. Somehow, the Sisters managed to draw most of the ramblings back to faith and God.

I could not believe this woman had allowed five complete strangers into her home and was now giving them what was surely food she couldn't afford to give. Camino told me later that when most people give, their hearts naturally open up. This was an opportunity for the Sisters to go deeper and help those they encountered grow stronger in their faith. It was actually pretty incredible to witness what took place.

The nuns did confess to me later that sometimes they would go hours without anyone answering the door or inviting them in. This meant they would go hungry, and that was the most intriguing part of my conversation with them. They believed the suffering they endured as a result could be offered up to God, because they more closely resembled Jesus in his poverty and suffering.

I wasn't sure what to think about that, but then they shared that they also believed their suffering could bring about as much or even more good than if they had shared a meal with someone like Esther. I had no clue what they were talking about, because it didn't make sense to me at all. How could not eating be seen as a good thing? And how could suffering result in anything positive? And if God was so wonderful and their prayers so powerful, why would he allow them to go without food?

Chapter 32

THE TRUTH ABOUT
SUFFERING #1

When we arrived back at the Sisters' house, they hugged us and thanked us for joining them. Then they wished us well and actually broke into song as we got into Camino's car. It seemed a bit too out-of-this-world for me, and I was still trying to process what had happened that night at Esther's house. If I'd been an emotional guy, I might've been moved to tears at their beautiful singing. They seemed so loving and real. And sincerely at peace despite their self-induced suffering.

"Okay, Camino, so you've gotta help me with this," I started as soon as he backed out of the driveway. "I mean, how can suffering be good? I seriously don't get it." I realized I'd hardly allowed the car doors to shut before bombarding him with questions, but my mind couldn't wait.

"Well, Cleve, let's start by comparing pleasure to pain in worldly terms," Camino said. "The grief one suffers at the loss of a child surely outweighs the joy at that same child's birth. Loss gives us more pain than pleasure gives us joy."

"Uh, okay, I think I'm with you so far, but what does that have to do with those nuns?" I was practically begging for answers.

"The affliction of sickness far exceeds the pleasure of health," Camino continued. "An insult wounds us more than honor flatters us. Nature dispenses joys and sorrows so unequally that the latter affects us more powerfully than the former. This demonstrates the delusiveness of worldly happiness."

"You're losing me now," I said, shaking my head. "I don't usually have to think this much." I chuckled, but quieted when I realized Camino hadn't joined me.

"Your inability to understand how suffering can be good is a result of looking at the situation from the eyes of the world instead of the eyes of heaven," Camino said. "To the world, suffering is bad. To God, rightly intended and ordered, suffering can actually be good. Of course it isn't God who is causing our suffering. He simply allows it to happen so that we will derive a greater good from it. For instance, we can convert our setbacks into prayer, which can be incredibly powerful. In fact, prayer is our greatest weapon on earth."

"Cleve, life isn't about how much money you make or how fast you grow your business," Camino went on. "It isn't about how beautiful your wife is or how big your house is. It's about love, and the gift of self. It's about focusing on what really matters and remembering we are children of God."

Most of what he was saying was still going over my head, but I tried to make sense of it all. How could suffering and pain be good? I'd always equated pleasure with good, pain with bad. It's that simple, right? Seek pleasure; avoid pain.

Chapter 33

THE TRUTH ABOUT
SUFFERING #2

amino, you've got me really confused now," I admitted. "Am I getting this right—you're saying I would be happier if I suffered more? Bad things are actually good things? I mean, I've understood a lot of what you said so far, but this right here makes no sense at all." Maybe I was being too blunt, but I couldn't help it. I really wanted to understand how he could be sincere in this belief.

"Here's the deal, Cleve," Camino said. "I know this is a hard one to grasp, and maybe I should've left it for a later lesson, but once you get this . . . I mean, once you make this concept your own, the joy you can experience is immeasurable. Let's try this: If something good happens to you, you are happy, right?"

I nodded. I could agree with that at least. "If you eat or drink something you love, you experience pleasure. Correct?" Again, I nodded, thinking of a juicy T-bone cooked to the perfect temp.

"Okay, and the logical, typical response to pain or doing things we don't like is sadness or depression or unhappiness or whatever you want to call it," Camino said.

Still nodding in agreement, I felt like we were finally getting somewhere. But how did that connect to what we'd just been talking about?

"What if we turned this thinking upside down?" Camino's question caught me by surprise. "We would still find enjoyment in the good things, but what if we could also find happiness in our struggles? What if the pain we experienced could be looked at in such a way as to also bring us happiness?"

"Now I'm back to being confused, Camino," I said dryly. "So everything should make us happy, whether it's good or bad?"

"I'm not suggesting the impossible," Camino said. "I'm not saying we could remove all sadness or avoid periods where something bad wouldn't affect us negatively at all. But what if, after an appropriate amount of time, we were able to view these 'setbacks' as loving gestures? What if we could generally have this perspective? Wouldn't it be logical to assume we'd be happier? I mean, nothing would get us down for long."

I was pondering his words, rolling them around in my head. It didn't sound completely ridiculous, but I still wasn't convinced. Camino didn't wait for a response from me, but continued on.

"So, this line of thinking is logical, but it also presents the power of a divine perspective; one where we secure the belief that everything happens for a reason," he said. "There's even a verse in your own Bible that I could show you that says that very thing, but I'll get to that later. I want you to grasp this, because that which may at first seem bad can actually be turned around for your benefit. To go back to our baseball analogy, even when you fly out, you can still drive in a run for your team. That's why they call it a sacrifice fly."

Chapter 34

DETACH

I t sounded pretty blissful the way he said it, but I was still struggling with it all. His stance conflicted with everything I knew to be true. I don't remember ever hearing anyone talk about suffering as being a good thing, although Mother Teresa came to mind almost immediately as I thought about this whole idea. She lived with next to nothing and devoted her whole life to the diseased and dying. Two of my favorite quotes from her that my Mom had on her bedroom wall were, "Every time you smile at someone, it is an action of love, a gift to that person, a beautiful thing." And "If you judge people, you have no time to love them." She was an amazing lady.

I was at a conference once where she gave a talk, and there was a special spark about her. Even with everything she suffered through, I could tell she was doing exactly what she was supposed to be doing in life. "Camino, I'll be honest," I said. "I'm still struggling with this concept, but I'm trying to wrap my mind around it. I think I'm getting closer."

"How about this? Why don't you live this concept for a week and see what happens," Camino suggested. "Sometimes a firsthand experience is the best way to fully understand a new concept. What do you think?"

What was I going to say? No? I couldn't say that, after everything he was trying to do for me. "Sure," I said simply.

"Alright then, this week's assignment is a bit different," Camino said. "In a sense, I don't want you to *do* anything. I want you *not* to do some things. Give up a few things you like doing. Suffer a bit."

Uh-oh, I sure didn't like the sound of this. I must've had my thoughts clearly written across my face, because Camino hurried on.

"It's hard to know joy when you don't know pain," Camino said. "It's hard to learn what really matters until you give up a few things you think *do* matter, but really don't. Suffering is a reality of this world. The joyful soul embraces it."

"Well, maybe I don't really want to be joyful, if it means giving up stuff I like to do," I answered smartly.

"Those who don't embrace it may experience some happiness, but they rarely will understand authentic joy,"

Camino pressed further. "I can't say any more than this right now. There is much more to learn before I can say all I have to share with you. Just remember the Sisters, Cleveland. Have you ever seen happier human beings? Yet even meeting the basic need of food to eat is a daily self-imposed challenge for them."

I sighed. I knew he was going to bring those nuns up again, and he was right. They had seemed pretty happy. I had to admit, they'd seemed to have something I don't think I've ever experienced.

"Their answer to whether they find a meal or not is the same: joy. Joy in sharing a meal and joy in suffering when not having a meal," Camino said. "Now Cleve, I'm not saying you can't have fun and enjoy many of the things this world has to offer. But you must strive to maintain the proper perspective. The pleasures of this world are mostly fleeting. The joys of the next world endure, so the less we focus and the more we detach from this world, the more we will be prepared for the next world."

Whoa, now he was talking crazy talk. *The next world?* I wasn't sure what I believed about that either, but I didn't think I could handle all that along with everything I was already trying to work on right now. My goal was to live the American dream. This meant freedom, having nice things, and going to nice places. Why should I limit this? What good would that even do?

"So Camino, I have to admit, this is starting to sound a little depressing," I said. "Basically you are saying I think I am happy but I'm not? Or I'm lying to myself? Besides, why would I want to limit what I've rightfully earned? I mean, I understand why the nuns do what they do, but they live a special life and seem to have some kind of calling to do that kind of thing. I live in the real world and it's a lot different."

Camino's next question told me he'd clearly been expecting me to push back on this one. And darn it if he didn't start to win me over with the right question. "So Cleve, what is it that makes you successful?" he said with an air of satisfaction as we pulled up next to my car.

Chapter 35

THE FIRST BATTLE
OF THE WILL

I don't know, Camino," I admitted. "I suppose being competitive, wanting to win. Doing things others aren't willing to do. Plus, I'm good at running things, like my business."

"There is one key word you mentioned," Camino responded. "We'll likely get into it in a future lesson, but it doesn't hurt to cover it a bit here. You said the word 'willing.' Remember when we spoke about thinking and feeling and doing? Well, the will is all about the doing. Our thinking and feeling can be totally on track, but until this translates into doing, nothing actually gets done. Utilizing our willpower is what sacrifice is all about. It's almost entirely a function of your will."

"I guess I can understand that," I agreed. "I mean, if I'm giving up something I like it would have to be willingly, since no one's going to force me and tell me to give it up."

"Exactly," Camino said with a smile. "Your will is like a muscle. It needs to be exercised to make it stronger. You've made sacrifices to become good at what you do. You go beyond what others expect of you, and this strength comes from your will to win. But with regular exercise your will can become even stronger. Allow me to give you one simple example: When, in the course of a day, is the first battle of your will?"

"Hmm . . . that's a tough one," I said. "I guess I would say when I'm trying to get my kids ready for school." Although to be honest, I didn't help Cindy that much with the kids.

"I would contend your first battle comes quite a bit before that," Camino said confidently.

"Before that? Okay, I give up then," I said.

"Out of curiosity, how many times do you hit the snooze button on your alarm clock before you get out of bed?" He tilted his head in that way that told me he already knew the answer.

"Whoa, that's getting a little personal, and besides, what does that have to do with anything?" I felt my hackles rising again. "I'm not a morning person, so I'm not always ready to just jump out of bed. I'm really more of a night person."

"So I take it you, like many people, are getting trounced in the first battle of the will each day," Camino said. "And I know to you it might sound silly, but if you can win this first battle, you will get some early momentum to help you defeat others throughout the day. I challenge you not to hit the snooze button and determine right now that you will get up and out of bed the minute your alarm goes off. You might be surprised at how an early win like this can set a positive tone for the day."

"That's my homework assignment? Don't hit the snooze button?" I almost sneered but thought better of it. "Sounds pretty ridiculous."

"Think of it this way, Cleve," Camino said. "When you set the time on your alarm to get up, you are requesting yourself to get up at that time."

"Wait, so you're saying when I hit the snooze I am basically ignoring a request that I scheduled with myself?" The light was dawning a bit.

"Absolutely! Now you're getting it!" Camino was excited now. "In a sense, you are a no-show for an appointment that you scheduled with yourself. Plus, you have given into laziness and comfort. I could go on a bit more and we could talk about vices, but once again, I'm getting ahead of myself. Let's stick to next week's assignment, which actually includes three other challenges. Here they are:"

Chapter 36

ASSIGNMENT #2

"1. Get up as soon as your alarm goes off.

2. No baseball games.

3. No alcohol.

4. Zero late nights getting home."

Holy cow, he was taking this way too far! Maybe I could do one of those, but all four of them in one week? That's like setting myself up for failure. "Camino, come on," I protested. "Baseball games and hitting

Ted's on my way home are my outlets. These are things I need to do to survive the cutthroat world of owning a small business. I'll end up having a terrible week or a nervous breakdown. But even more than that, I simply can't leave the office at five o'clock like every other employee. I have way too much responsibility and several people are counting on me. Plus, I have to set the tone in my office. If the owner leaves early, it implies it's okay for everyone else to go home early too."

After a moment, Camino said, "First of all, Cleve, I'm just asking you to do this for one week. We can tweak things as we go. Secondly, think of this like a battle. A competition that you must win. In this case, it's a legitimate battle against yourself. You think you can't do it?" He paused.

"It's not that I *can't* do it," I began, and then stopped. Man, this guy was good. Now he had me mad because he was insinuating that I didn't believe I could do it. I can't stand losing. Ever. He couldn't have hit a more perfect home run.

He continued, "Cleve, I'm curious. What time do you consider too early to leave the office?"

"Any time before 5:30 p.m."

"And how many times after that time do you make major decisions or get more work done than before that time?" He wasn't going to let up.

"Honestly, most of the time, everything is done, but this time allows me to get caught up on things from the chaos of the day," I answered.

"Why are your days chaotic?" Camino asked.

"Really? You just asked that? I own a small business. It's just the nature of business, Camino."

"But does it always have to be that way? I mean, aren't there people to help and systems that can be implemented to cut down on chaos? Have you heard of the difference between activity and productivity?" Camino was animated again.

Chapter 37

ACTIVE VERSUS PRODUCTIVE

E   nlighten me," I said with a touch of sarcasm. Who was he to question my work ethic or ability to set my business up for success? I work hard. And since it's up to me to succeed or fail, I'm not going to stop working hard just because of what Camino might think.

"Maybe the best way to explain it is to give you another example," Camino said. "Let's say I'm assembling cars with a faulty tool. I work really hard to get as many cars out the door as

I can, but it is clear the tool is holding me back from producing as many as I could. So, to watch me work, you would think I was working incredibly hard. I was very 'active' all day. But at the end of the day, was I as 'productive' as I could've been if I had used a good tool?"

"Well, no," I admitted. Once again, I sensed I knew where this was going, but I let Camino continue. He seemed to enjoy hearing himself talk.

"Another way to think about this is from a reactive versus proactive standpoint," Camino said. "Or even defense versus offense. At the end of the day, when you look back on what was accomplished, it is important to regularly assess how many of your activities pushed the needle forward on accomplishing your goals. Ask yourself these questions: How many of your activities accentuated your strengths; how many were of your choosing versus being chosen for you; and how many were truly productive, producing your best work?"

Right away I could think of a few things that jumped to mind that might be wasting my time. How could this guy be right so much of the time?

"The beauty of this line of thinking is that it can allow you to generate hours back into your life," Camino continued. "To be your best self, ideally, you should focus most of your time and energy on activities that make your heart sing."

"Okay, this is getting a little sappy," I joked. "Is there a method where I get to keep my man card?"

"Cleve, I'm serious," Camino said. "The things you focus on should allow you to best utilize your talent and, if possible, you should surround yourself with people whose talents complement your weaknesses."

"Well, that makes sense and doesn't sound so girly," I said, grinning at him.

Chapter 38

TALENT AND BALANCE

A t some point we need to do a full assessment of your talents and the talents of your team, but for now, the main concern is giving up some things," Camino went on.

I was envisioning myself in a chair in a dark room. A bright light was shining in my face and there were wires attached to my forehead. Hopefully it was just my imagination running wild and not a foreshadowing of this "assessment" he was referring to, but nonetheless, it sounded strange.

"Cleve?" I snapped back from my reverie. Camino had still been talking. "What do you think about this?"

"Ah, I think it all sounds good," I said, not really knowing what he was referring to.

He raised an eyebrow and I knew I'd been caught. It was seventh grade history all over again. "Worldly pleasures and success rarely shape who we are nor does it result in true joy," Camino said. "We have to strive for balance. Virtue is found in the middle of extremes, as is courage found between recklessness and timidity. Natural setbacks will take place, and as long as we realize that and don't punish ourselves for it, success is in our reach. Does this all sound doable to you?"

"I believe so, Camino," I answered. "At least I know what you want me to try to do. The execution may be a bit difficult."

"I'm glad you brought that up," Camino said. Of course he was. This guy had an answer for everything. "It's okay to miss a few opportunities to challenge yourself in these areas. Be ready for it. You might win some battles, but the war is ongoing. The key is to continue to fight hard with every skirmish. Try to picture yourself as the king of a castle surrounded by a moat and protected by a strong drawbridge. While these represent a formidable defense, you also have troops further out scouting to see if enemies are approaching. The goal is to fight your battles as far away from your castle as possible. You will lose some battles, but you have to keep fighting even when your back is against the wall. Don't let yourself get down for long or else the enemy could get past your moat and throw ladders against your castle and really wreak havoc. Make sense?"

My eyes must have been glazed over, because Camino hurried on.

"I know this is a lot to take in. I might have gone a bit far with the castle analogy. Just work the plan I have provided and don't hesitate to call me if you need me. Otherwise, I'll see you next week."

That was it. All that talking and now he was just sitting there, waiting for me to get in my car and just drive home. Sighing, I closed my door and rested my head against the seat for a moment. My drive home wasn't going to be long enough to process all this new information.

Chapter 39

THE BATTLE BEGINS

O f all the things Camino could have picked. I seriously can't stand my alarm clock. As an entrepreneur, I don't really *have* to get up. But I have always felt the need to set it and at least do my part in the morning with the kids despite the fact that Cindy usually has everything covered. I really hate that sound—the one that stubbornly insists I get up and out of my nice, warm bed. Its one redeeming quality was something I was now supposed to avoid: the snooze button.

Dang it. I loved those quiet nine-minute mindless intervals of thoughts and dreams, and it really felt like I was getting much-needed sleep. I've always found it interesting that all alarm clocks picked that interval for snoozing. I discovered recently that it all dates back to the original digital clocks. They could only track one digit, so in a sense, it couldn't think past nine. And I, in turn, felt like I couldn't start thinking until nine snoozes had gone by! Okay, that's an exaggeration, but there were days when I hit it multiple times.

So where does this leave me? Cursing, of course. Cursing Camino for suggesting I had to give up the snooze. I love my snooze button. It was not nice at all for him to insist I do that. But of course, my competitive nature wouldn't let the snooze button win. I had to prove I could do it. And so I did. But no one said I had to be happy about it. Alright, so I'd won the first battle of my will. I was feeling pretty successful, and I knew it was going to be a great day. Or so I thought.

So, now that I was actually up at five-thirty on a Saturday morning, what was I going to do with myself? It was too early to cut the grass. The neighbors would kill me. As I popped a piece of bread into the toaster, the dishwasher caught my eye. *Should I?* Well, I might as well get started on this whole challenge thing. I opened the dishwasher and realized one very important thing: I had no idea where most of this stuff went.

Fifteen minutes later, I was enjoying my cold toast. I'd done it. Sure, Cindy was going to wonder where her favorite lasagna pan was because I was pretty sure I hadn't put it in the proper place, but I'd done a decent job. Plates, cups, bowls, and silverware were simple. That whisk thing? Not so easy. I sipped the coffee I'd brewed myself. It tasted terrible. But I had made it.

Chapter 40

RECONNECTING

C indy shuffled into the kitchen and stopped; her jaw dropped. Her robe was tied loosely at her waist. I could tell she'd slept on her right side, facing away from me, as had become her habit several years ago. Her hair was completely flat on the right and sticking almost straight out on the left. Since she usually beat me out of bed, I didn't normally see her this way.

My eyes met hers over my coffee mug. The look on her face was enough to have me swallowing a giggle, but I couldn't mask the smile that crossed my face. Cindy was cute before she'd had her coffee. I'd almost forgotten that.

She shoved one hand through her hair, managing to tangle it even more as a quizzical look formed in her eyes. "Cleve? Do you have an early meeting?" The confusion was evident as she made her way to the dishwasher. I didn't know what she was doing, but when she opened it and stood, staring, I couldn't help it. I felt like the proverbial cat that swallowed the canary.

"No, Cindy, no meeting today," I answered. "As a matter of fact, I don't think I'm going into the office today at all."

Now she turned, eyes widened, as I grinned at her. "What's going on here?" She had an accusatory tone, which made me chuckle out loud. "Did *you* unload the dishes?"

"I might have," I said mysteriously. "Good luck finding your pan and the inside of that crock pot thing when you need it. I had no idea where they went. Sorry."

"Sorry?" She was still facing me, but now she had an empty mug in her hands. "Seriously, Cleveland, what are you up to? Did you decide to take a last-minute trip with the guys this weekend?" She was pouring the coffee now, but one careful sip had her nose wrinkling in disgust. Bless her, she kept her mouth shut and came to sit across from me. As she did so, her robe slid from one shoulder.

"No, ah, I've got, um, no plans with the guys," I stammered, my gaze skittering away from her bare shoulder. She wasn't wearing a particularly revealing nightgown, but I was, after all, a man, and the passion in our relationship had dimmed in pretty much every area, if you get what I mean.

She glanced down and yanked her robe up to her neck when she noticed it sagging off her shoulder. I was almost disappointed.

"Okay, well, do you have a major yard project planned then?" She'd managed to gulp down more coffee, but I noticed the sugar packets she'd emptied into her mug while I was up for a refill. Her eyes seemed a bit more focused, so I figured now was a good time to bring up my idea.

"As a matter of fact, I do plan to cut the grass early this morning, but I knew the Morgans would be upset if I got started before eight, so I'm holding off for a bit. But I was thinking. You know how we used to go to the driving range when the kids were little?"

Chapter 41

SETTING A DATE
WITH THE FAM

Yeah, we'd go there and smack some balls around together; then you'd head off to a golf game and we'd go home," she said, a tinge of jealousy in her voice. "Brian had fun, even though Jenna was small enough to nap the whole time in the stroller."

"Right, I remember that," I said quickly, although to be honest, I didn't. "Well, anyway, what if the four of us go to the driving range for an hour or so this afternoon?"

"Got a golf game later?" Cindy was curious, but was once again surprised when I shook my head.

"Nope, just want to go have some fun with my family," I answered, enjoying the look on her face. It was kind of fun to watch all the emotions cross her expression. Surprise, disbelief, pleasure, suspicion. They were all there. Had I really been that much of a jerk?

"Oh I get it," she said finally. "You've got a potential client meeting you there and you want to wine and dine him with Cleve the 'family man.' No thanks. I've got flowerbeds to weed, and I need to polish the silver."

Boy, if that didn't sound like a made-up excuse. I usually saw her polish the silver once a year, and it certainly wasn't time for that. "Cindy, I'm serious," I pleaded. I realized now how badly I actually wanted to go do this with them. "Please, I have no ulterior motive. I just want to do something with you guys."

One eyebrow raised, she glanced toward the entryway of our kitchen as Brian stumbled in. "What's with all the talking out here so early on a Saturday?" He rubbed his eyes and then stopped short.

"Dad?" The shock had his voice tapering off in a shrill squeak. *Oh brother.* He was probably getting to that age where he'd start to grow some chest hair and need the full "talk" pretty soon.

"Your father wants to take us to the driving range this afternoon," Cindy said. "Want to go hit some golf balls around?"

Brian's eyes lit. "Really? You mean it?" Cindy's look told me everything I needed to know. If I backed out now, she was going to strangle me in my sleep. I winked at her.

"Sure, Bri," I answered. "You, me, your mom, and your sister. How does that sound?"

"That sounds fun, I mean, um, yeah," Brian's voice calmed as he sauntered to the counter. He reached to the cabinet for a bowl before turning and nonchalantly stating. "Whatever."

Whatever? Where was the excitement from a moment ago? I looked back at Cindy, who shrugged. Well, okay, I could work with that. Jenna trudged into the kitchen a moment later, her braids frizzy from sleep.

"Daddy?" She also sounded surprised. Boy, I've been a real screw-up. Time to change that.

"Hey Jen-Jen," I said, using her pet name from years ago. "C'mere." I held out my arms, and after a brief glance at Cindy, she moved forward tentatively. I put my arm around her, afraid to commit to the whole "hugging thing" just yet. Didn't want to completely freak them out.

"Want to go with me and Bri and Mom to do something fun this afternoon?" I looked down into her sweet face. *How could I have ignored this for so long?* She's adorable, and the spitting image of her mother.

"Sure Daddy," Jenna said. She skipped to the dishwasher but turned when she found it empty. "Can someone get me a bowl?"

Cindy automatically stood, but I beat her to the punch. "Here ya go, Jenna," I said, giving her a bowl and a cup for her juice. Cindy was still shaking her head in disbelief while Brian attacked a bowl of granola.

Chapter 42

NOT-SO-GREEN THUMB

I puttered around in the garage for a bit, putting away a few things I'd left out the last time I'd done yard work. Then I came back in to check the time. Hmm . . . seven. Still too early to cut the grass. Then I got an idea.

A few minutes later, Cindy stepped out the front door. She had her gardening gloves on, she'd pulled her hair back into a smart-looking ponytail, and she was wearing a visor. She looked like she'd just stepped out of an ad in *Garden Beauties*. Okay, not quite, but heck, I was batting a thousand right now, so I was feeling pretty good. She stopped, the suspicious look back on her face. "Cleve? What are you doing?" She said the words slowly, as if I were holding a gun and she was the negotiator.

"I thought it was pretty obvious," I said. "I'm weeding the flowerbeds. Want to help? Or better yet, get a lawn chair and just sit and keep me company while I work."

"Cleve, I don't know what's going on, but whatever it is, you're coming on a little strong," she said, voicing her concern. "You can't just wake up one day and be a completely different person. Wait, don't pull that one. It's not a weed."

Moving forward, she joined me on her knees, pointing to the flowers that had just broken the surface. "Those are not weeds," she said. "Just these here."

"I promise, Cindy, I don't have an ulterior motive," I said. "But I think I may have pulled a few flowers." I grimaced as she rolled her eyes, but I was surprised when a light chuckle escaped her lips.

Later, I left her finishing the weeding while I cut the grass. When I got out of the shower after trimming the rosebush, she'd made lemonade. *Fresh-squeezed lemonade.* Just the way I like it. Whoa. Camino hadn't mentioned I'd get benefits for my efforts, but I guess it only made sense.

Chapter 43

FAMILY OUTING

I wish I could say the day had been perfect. Well, I guess I *could* say that, but it would be a lie. My old self had reared up at the driving range, correcting Brian and even Jenna on their form while hitting the ball. I don't know why I have such a hard time reading cues. Looking back I should have seen them getting more and more frustrated. And so I tried to rein it in, but my temper got the best of me and Brian had ended up throwing one of the rented drivers out on the course before heading to the car in a huff.

I'd had no choice but to go after it, dodging golf balls somewhat unsuccessfully the whole time. That had been the end of the trip to the driving range, and we'd ridden back in complete silence. When we got home, Brian had stomped off to his room and Cindy had given me that "look" she gets when I've really blown it. You know, the one that makes you feel like you're about two inches tall?

Sunday I hit the snooze before I even realized it, but only once. I was rather proud of myself, but when I realized I'd already missed going to church with the family, I sank back into bed. I'd wanted to surprise Cindy by attending Mass with them, but since I hadn't made it, what was the point of getting up now?

The rest of the day had been par for the course. Nothing new, nothing really happening, but I did watch the baseball game on television while sipping a beer.

Monday I was determined to get back on track. The morning at home went well. I got up on the first buzz of the alarm, then even managed to get the bottom rack of the dishwasher unloaded before Cindy caught me in the kitchen. I learned a valuable lesson through this process: There is always time to stop the snowball of negativity even after it starts rolling down the hill.

Chapter 44

SCREWUP

T hings began smoothly at the office as well. Until the end of the day, that is.

Bill stormed into my office at five minutes to five. "Cleve, what the heck is going on with Kepler?" His face and neck were beet red, and he was breathing heavily.

"I have no idea what you're talking about," I said cautiously. Chuck Kepler was our biggest account, representing almost 30 percent of our revenue. "What's the matter?"

"Well, Mr. Fancy Pants Fred over there on your welding team didn't weld the axle rods correctly on their last order," Bill answered, spit flying as he bit off each word. "They're all falling apart, and Chuck just called me himself. I had to wipe my ear after the call because of all the yelling from his end."

"Oh man, okay, sorry," I said. Hastily, I added, "I'll call him back first and then deal with Fred. Is Fred still here? Does he know about this?"

"He's still here, and no, he has no clue," Bill said sharply.

Well, so much for getting out of here on time. After calling Chuck Kepler back and eating crow as well as crediting him for his last order, I tracked Fred down to tell him the good news. Actually, there *was* no good news. I planned on firing him, and I was about to do just that when his wife pulled in to pick him up with their four kids in tow. Dang it.

As his wife smiled and waved at us through the glass partition, I turned back to Fred. He'd never made a mistake like this before. "What's the deal, Fred?" I looked him in the eye. He stood, putting his back to the glass wall separating us from his family.

"We just lost a baby," he began, his throat thick with tears he was attempting to hold back. "We thought we were past the tough part, but we weren't. It was a boy." He pressed his fingers to his eyes.

I was in shock. I could see his pretty wife, struggling to keep control of their three oldest daughters while the youngest little girl was on her hip. This had been Fred's chance for a boy. Stunned, I did the only thing I could. I stammered out an apology.

"Fred, I'm so sorry," I said. "I do know what it feels like. Cindy and I suffered a loss like that back in the early days. That's rough."

"Yeah, thanks," Fred choked out. I could tell he was trying to hold it together for the family watching him through the glass. "We actually named him Peter, and we even had a small funeral for him just a few days ago."

"Really?" It was out before I could filter my response. "I mean, uh, I didn't know they did that sort of thing for miscarriages."

"He was twenty-three weeks, and his lungs hadn't formed properly, but when he was born he was so perfect and tiny I couldn't just let them take him away," Fred whispered, his voice rough with emotion.

"Oh man, I don't know what to say," I said. I truly was at a loss for words. I couldn't fire this guy. He was going through something terrible right now, and as much as I wanted to have someone to hang the disaster on, I couldn't hold it against him right now.

"Cleve, I swear this will never happen again," Fred apologized. "You know I'd never knowingly put out something that wasn't completely up to par. I must've been distracted with what we were dealing with. We knew for a day or so that Julia was going to have to deliver a stillborn baby, and I guess I should've asked for the day off."

"Yes, you should've," I said. I believed his sincere apology and his promise. He'd never given me reason to believe otherwise. And although it was a costly mistake, it was certainly something any one of us could've done. "Alright, Fred, it's done, it's over with, and I think you should take some time with your family. I can't give you the week off with full pay, but I could give you the rest of this week at half pay, if you want to take advantage of it, spend some time with Julia and your girls?"

"Really? Uh, wow, Cleve, I wouldn't have thought you would ever . . ." he trailed off, as if he realized how he sounded.

"Don't look a gift horse in the mouth, Fred," I said with a chuckle. "Go on. Go home." I walked him out, met his wife and girls, and checked my watch. Crap. It was twenty to six. Battle lost. Well, I was late anyway. I might as well stop at Ted's, since I'd had such a crummy afternoon. I really needed that vodka. And really, stopping for just one drink would still be a vast improvement from normal. I could still get home by sevenish.

Chapter 45

ONE AND DONE

ow, Cleve, one and done?" Ted's surprise was
evident as I stood, throwing my card down with
the tab. As he brought the receipt for me to sign,
he looked at me quizzically. "What's gotten into you?"

"Just trying to cut back a bit," I answered. I wasn't ready to
share about my "new self" just yet.

"Really? Since when?" He took the receipt and wiped the
counter down, removing my glass as I headed toward the door.

"Since today, really," I said, backing away a few steps. Man, I was nervous about going home. Maybe I should get another one, just to settle my nerves. No, I have to be done.

"You know I love your gimlets, man, but I'm trying to stay focused a bit more at home," I said. That wasn't the whole truth, but I didn't want to try to explain it more, and I was worried I'd end up having another drink. For all the times I've cried on Ted's shoulder, I just didn't believe the way I was thinking would make sense to him. Maybe I was wrong, but I just didn't feel like baring my soul to him tonight.

"Alright," Ted said, raising one hand in a salute. "You do what you gotta do!"

"Thanks, Ted. See you soon." As I pushed the door open, I was struck with guilt that I had stopped there at all. But, I reasoned, it was pretty great that I'd stopped at just one drink. Come to think of it, I don't think I've *ever* stopped at just one drink before. Huh. That's something to chew on later.

Chapter 46

SURPRISE!

W ow, you're home early!" Cindy was wearing the apron her mom had worn, and she spun around when I entered the room. "Seven?" She looked at the clock on the microwave as if she didn't believe.

Huh. I leave work late, stop for a drink, and I'm still considered early when I get home. Never gave it much thought, but how late did I usually come home? "I'm a changed man, Cindy," I quipped. I suddenly realized I wanted that statement to be real.

"Sure you are, Cleve," she laughed. "Now, why don't you go change into your work clothes and fix the doorknob the dog ruined last week while I was at work?"

"Okay." That was it. I did exactly what she asked. Without hesitation and without expecting anything in return. And yet I did get something in return: a very appreciative wife.

She kissed me full on the mouth when she walked into the hall and saw I was actually doing what she asked. "Maybe you *are* a changed man," she said with wonder in her voice. "I think I'm going to make a list of some other things we need done around here."

I didn't really even hear her. I was still reeling from her kiss. Cindy had rarely ever instigated physical affection, even back in the early days of our marriage. I shook my head as I continued to work. This will and virtue stuff just might be paying off! I know that's not really the point, but still, I couldn't help but wonder what else I could do to get that response from her. I had heard the saying "Happy wife; happy life" before, but I had never really believed it could be that simple.

Chapter 47

WEEKLY STATUS REPORT

S o I won and lost some battles this week. For some reason it proved more difficult to give things up than add things. Here's my tally for the week:

I only left work by five-thirty twice. Not the best, but this week was legitimately insane. And I don't believe I have the team in place to alleviate this anytime soon. But then again, I suppose that is more of an excuse because I obviously have the power to make the necessary improvements. This made me think of something a colleague had told me one time:

"Cleve, never forget you are completely in charge. You own the company. Make the tough decisions you have to make in the best interests of the company. And ultimately these will be in your best interests as well."

I only stopped by Ted's twice all week! It hurt Ted's business a bit, but let's face it, if he was relying on my gimlets every night as his bread and butter, he was heading for a meager retirement anyway. Maybe I could get by with once or twice a week and I could still get stuff off my chest there while not spending all my extra time (and money) at Ted's.

The baseball team was on the road this week, so that one was easy. Not sure if I'd have managed to avoid a game if they'd been in town, but hey, a victory was a victory.

And finally, the dreaded alarm clock. I went four for seven. I didn't think weekends should count, but Saturday I had gotten up right when it went off. Tuesday had been rough after the shock from Fred's situation and Friday was just the end of a rough week. I did only hit the snooze once on Tuesday, so that should count for something. Thursday night the dog had been a complete nuisance all night, whining and trying to get in bed with Cindy and me, so I felt like I deserved an extra nine minutes Friday morning.

Overall, I thought things had gone fairly well.

Chapter 48

MEETING #3

"ey Camino, how's it going?" I briskly walked to what was becoming "our" table at Cliff's, shook his hand, and slid into the booth opposite him.

"It's going great, Cleve, but I've taken on a few more challenging assignments lately, so any prayers you could send my way to help would be much appreciated," Camino said with a smile.

"Will do." Like I pray. I snorted inwardly. Oh well—he'd never know. "So what could be more challenging than me?" I held my hands out and then pointed my thumbs back at myself as I grinned.

"How did this week go?" He ignored my question, so I launched into a diatribe of the week, highlighting my wins and glossing over the losses. "Did you have any challenges?"

"I found it was harder to stop behaviors than to start new ones," I answered honestly. Camino was nodding as I continued. "For example, it was sort of easy to just follow through and do what Cindy asked me to do right away when she asked, but it was much harder to stop working and leave on time."

"What did you find most challenging?" Camino leaned forward, putting his elbows on the table after the server left with our order. He sipped his sweet tea while he listened.

"The snooze button was the hardest," I admitted. "But then again, it also seems like it's the most insignificant."

"Don't want to argue, but it's actually one of the most important things to get right in this whole deal," he said, sitting back again, his arms over his chest. "Remember, it's the first battle of the will. So it starts you off on the right foot and likely helps you win a few more battles throughout the day."

I could see his point. I usually could. "Okay, I get it, and seriously, I did try," I said. "I managed to get up right away four times out of seven, so I don't think that's too bad. I have a question for you now. What about weekends on that deal? Or what about a night where sleep is interrupted? Would I still have to get up right away?"

Camino speared some lettuce, dipping it in his dressing and taking his time chewing while he thought it over. "Good question. It depends. Most folks find getting up at the same time every day to be a great habit to keep regardless of whether their sleep was perfect the night before or not," he said. "Now, certainly, there have to be some exceptions. And for these times, perhaps you could set your alarm to go off a bit later. But whatever you decide to do, set your intentions and follow through. Stick to it. As for weekends, you are clearly free to do what you want, but again, I find it best to maintain the practice."

"That sounds fair," I said. "I'm not sure I'll be good at it, but I might experiment with it a bit. After all, I did get up right away last Saturday and I got the dishwasher unloaded, had breakfast with my wife after shocking her silly, and did some weeding all before the time I would normally get up. I guess I could also use that extra time to get a head start on my business week or catch up on stuff I had to let go so I could leave on time during the week."

I'd heard of other successful businesspeople doing this and I'd always thought it was crazy. Why would I want to bring work home on the weekends? Isn't that why I have an office at work? Supposedly, though, just an hour or two early on Saturday mornings helped them get a head start on a project or plan out their week. Hard to argue it wouldn't be time well spent. Especially for someone like me since I like to fly by the seat of my pants.

"Cleve?" I snapped back into focus, realizing Camino had been trying to get my attention for a few seconds before I responded. "Your burger is getting cold, buddy."

"Yeah, yeah, okay," I said. I could tell he was about to lay a big one on me. I braced myself inwardly.

"So, here's the million-dollar question, Cleveland," Camino started. Uh-oh, I hated when people used my full name. With both my mom and Cindy, it meant I was in trouble. "What did you learn from your small sacrifices?"

Chapter 49

SACRIFICIAL LEARNING

The knee-jerk truth? It felt like I hadn't learned all that much, so I answered as honestly as I could. "I'm not sure I learned anything too profound other than how to make my wife want to kiss me more often." I grinned, but Camino didn't share my reaction.

"Well then, this is a bit disappointing," Camino said. My stomach dropped. I hated losing, remember?

"Hey, I think I did pretty good," I protested.

"Now, now, don't get bent out of shape," Camino said. "I said it was disappointing, but it's not surprising either. It's hard for most to fully comprehend how self-imposed sacrifices actually can make life better. But it's true. Not only because it prepares you for when you have what is often called a 'passive contradiction,' meaning a bad experience not of your choosing, such as getting stuck behind a slow car when late or spilling ketchup on your shirt in the middle of the workday, but it also allows you the chance to build stronger relationships with those around you. Speaking of relationships, did your coming home on time have any positive effects on your family?"

"Well, at first Cindy was very surprised," I admitted. "And although I didn't come home right at five-thirty every night, I *was* earlier than normal every single night, so by tonight I think she's going to be expecting it. I think it's obvious to her that I am working on some things. In fact, she did mention it. And now that I think about it, she's been nicer to me too."

"Excellent." Camino was smiling now. "What else?"

"Wednesday night she made beef stroganoff, which is one of my favorites, and she rarely makes it," I said, ticking off her pleasant responses on my hand. "And then of course, there was a kiss or two in there that felt totally random, and she did smile a lot more this week."

"Great! The better your relationship with your wife, the better all of the other relationships will be, especially at home," Camino encouraged. "Keep it up!"

"I was just thinking the ole 'happy wife; happy life' thing might really be true, huh?" I could tell Camino was genuinely pleased, whether he was pleased for me or with me, I didn't know, nor did I care. I just knew this all felt good. A little bit like the day I made my first real sale.

He brought me right back down to earth with his next question though. "Did you have any passive contradictions this week? In other words, did anything not go as planned? And if so, how did you handle it?"

Chapter 50

PASSIVE
CONTRADICTION

R eally? Build me up to tear me down? "Well, it's funny that you should ask that," I said. "Saturday, since I decided not to go into the office, I surprised the family and took them to the driving range. It's something we did a few times when the kids were really little, and I thought we'd enjoy it. However, I couldn't keep from correcting Brian, that's my son, when he was working on his swing. We got in a fight, and it pretty much ended there."

"Mmm," Camino was nodding again, his chin resting on his hands as he thought about what I'd shared. "How were things with Brian the rest of the week?"

"Well, he pretty much avoided me for a couple of days, but he seemed to loosen up by Wednesday, which is when I finally sucked it up and apologized for losing my temper on Saturday," I admitted.

"Okay, well, that's progress," he said. "What else? What about work?"

"I did have a pretty big issue come up that was out of my control," I said. "One of my employees made a huge mistake on an order, and as a result, my partner got chewed out by the client, I got chewed out by my partner and the client, and I was about to fire the employee for the mistake. It cost us a ton of money to win the client back."

"Well, what happened?" Camino was forking up salad again as I talked. I popped a french fry in my mouth before continuing.

"I talked to Fred, the employee responsible for the screw-up, and found out he and his wife had just been through a really rough patch where they lost a child, and it clearly had affected his ability to do his job," I said. "So I ended up giving him another chance; plus I told him to take the rest of the week off with half pay to be with his family."

"Whoa, are you getting soft?" Camino was almost chuckling. Almost. I realized I felt pretty good about what I'd done.

"What?" I squirmed. "No one's ever accused me of being soft."

"Well, what message does this send to the others on the team then?"

"Hopefully it shows them that we all make mistakes and I'm willing to forgive them if they don't make the same mistake twice and commit to doing better," I said. "And Fred was clearly sorry. I believed him when he said it wouldn't happen again. But that *is* the reason I was late getting home that particular night."

"Do you think your ability to deal with this issue in a calmer way had anything to do with having to deal with all the things you gave up this week?"

"Now that's a stretch, Camino," I answered. "I don't really see the connection at this point, but I suppose anything's possible."

"Fair enough," Camino said. "I know from experience that the two are indeed intertwined. But again, I also know it's hard to see at first. All in due time, my friend. Please keep in mind that even though we are breaking challenges into separate weeks, these principles and the actions you've taken are meant to carry over from week to week. We can always make some tweaks, but the key is to get started and then increase momentum as best you can. I'm not going to sugarcoat it, though. It can be like rolling a large ball up a hill. You can't turn your back or let go in any way or else 'your progress' could roll all the way back down the hill. And even though you have been rewarded for your efforts, you will still be tempted to give up some of what you have gained. It's human nature."

"Whoa, now, wait a minute," I protested. "I am happy with the way some of this is going, but I thought I only had to give this stuff up for a week."

"Okay, say you go back to what you were doing before," Camino suggested. "Do you see how it would affect your wife? Your son? The guys at work?"

"Well, I guess, I mean, yeah, but I don't know if I can give it all up all the time," I said.

"Some you don't have to. You are free to change your 'set' sacrifices. But some you should consider keeping forever. This is something we can discuss and adjust as need be. It's a work in progress. And I know you are willing to work on this, right?" Camino had his eyebrows raised in challenge again.

"Sure, alright, yeah, I guess so," I answered.

Chapter 51

PRINCIPLE #3

Good. It's time to move on to our next point," Camino began. "Just to recap, the first week you made some nice strides in virtue and more specifically in charity with your wife. Hopefully you also grew in understanding objective truths and how important it is to both know this and act on it. Last week I think you got a glimpse of how sacrificing and suffering can actually be a good thing, and while I admit it was an extreme example, you saw this first-hand from our experience with the Sisters."

I was nodding, my mouth crammed full of bacon burger. "Now we've arrived at possibly the most difficult concept," Camino said. I groaned. "Hold on, don't go getting all upset on me already. It's the real key to happiness, and yet almost every one of the so-called 'happiness gurus' gets it wrong. Or rather, leaves it out. As we discussed earlier, you are made of body and soul."

"Okay," I said slowly. I didn't know where this was going, but my crazy meter was signaling it could be off-the-charts strange.

"Just as your body needs to eat, so does your soul," Camino said. "Do you agree?"

"Sure." I had no idea what he was talking about.

"So, what do you think about prayer?" He just threw that out there. The question hung in the silence for a moment.

"Well, we've talked about this before," I said. "Basically, I think it's okay. I mean, I don't pray all that much except for when I'm in really bad situations or really want something good to happen. Then I usually say a little prayer to make everything work out for me. So I do pray. I kind of doubt I'm being heard, but I still do it."

"Was there prayer in your house growing up?" Camino was nursing his tea now.

"Not really," I began. "Or wait a minute. Now that I think about it, I do remember my mom praying for a few things every now and then. I never heard my dad pray, or at least not that I can remember. I don't remember him asking for anything from anyone. He was a self-made man, and not too humble about it. He was rather cold, always in charge, and totally convinced about everything he knew and said."

"What do you mean by that?"

"I remember one time when I was very young and my parents had some friends over. One of the guys asked my Dad about his faith," I said. "My Dad told him he was an atheist. And that was the end of that."

"So obviously your father wasn't too religious, was he?" Camino leaned back as our server refilled his tea.

"Hardly," I chuckled.

"Supposedly kids are much more likely to quit practicing their faith later in life if their father doesn't practice his," Camino suggested. "This appears to be the case with you. And overall, you're not alone. You've already shared you do believe there is a God, which of course, is good, true and reasonable. By the way, you can check out Aristotelian and Thomistic metaphysics if you ever need help on the reasonable part. Candidly, I am glad we don't have to go there right now with you!"

Me, too!

"Here are a couple interesting facts," Camino continued. "A great majority of Americans align with your stance: They believe in God. However, almost half of this group do very little to seek God daily through prayer."

He let that thought simmer for a moment while I worked on the last of my fries. "In order to love God, you have to know God, and to know God, you have to seek God, and to seek God, you must pray," he said. "There's nothing more important to achieving authentic joy than this."

Hmm . . . baseball games, gimlets at Ted's, landing a big account, my flashy car, big vacations . . . all of these things gave me joy. I was so lost in thought I almost missed what he said next.

"So, we've arrived at the third point. Prayer."

Chapter 52

REACTION

W ait a minute, Camino," I protested. "You're saying I can't be happy without prayer?"

"That's exactly what I'm saying," Camino answered. He sounded totally legit too. As if he actually believed in what he was saying. "So Cleve, the thing here is that this is really a 'do' business rather than a 'tell' business. There aren't enough points or rationales or pitches or tag lines that I could show you to convince you of this truth."

Well, that certainly didn't sound like proof. It sounded like the opposite of proof, actually. Camino continued. "It's the most challenging part about being in my business. 'A man convinced against his will is of the same opinion still.'"

"Now I've heard that one before," I said, agreeing. "But what are you saying? You can't force me to pray or it isn't real?"

"Basically," Camino said, "you have to will it. You have to commit to giving prayer a real shot. Then we can circle back and you can tell me all the reasons I was wrong about it. But I know with all my heart that if you truly commit to daily prayer, your life will change drastically. You will begin to learn what real joy is."

"Whew! It's getting deep in here, Camino," I said, trying to laugh off the serious moment. He wasn't taking the bait, however.

"Lasting peace, lasting joy," Camino continued. "When you have a true connection with God, no one and nothing can knock you down. No bad day, no cranky person. Nothing will keep you down for long when you fully comprehend life on the supernatural plane."

"Holy cow, you're getting in way over my head," I said. "English please." I was trying to grasp what he was saying. The truth was, I'd never put stock in prayer making much of a difference. And I was already not looking forward to this week's homework.

"A prayer expert once said this life is like a bad night in a bad hotel," Camino said as his answer. "The pleasures of the body are fleeting and they will all seem insignificant when we realize what true joy is. The pleasures of the soul are lasting. And prayer is what we do to feed the soul."

"Okay," I said, nodding. I still wasn't sure why I was nodding, but he continued anyway.

"So, let's talk about what prayer really is," Camino said. "Remember when we talked about love and how we know we love others and they love us? While there are many definitions and types of love, they all boil down to engaging in a more meaningful relationship. When I asked you about how you know your son or wife loves you your answers were essentially about how they relate to you. This relating is always a choice based on thoughts and feelings. This is the best part of love- it is freely given. In other words, Cindy, Brian, and Jenna do not *have* to love you. They choose to."

"I bet sometimes it feels like they *have* to love me," I quipped, but Camino did not appreciate my flippant response. He chose to ignore it.

"That's the reason for this exercise," Camino continued. "Your relationships with your children and wife are very important, but they aren't the most critical to achieving authentic joy. The most important relationship is the one you have with God. And again, to gain a relationship with God, you must talk to Him. Give Him attention. And this means choosing to set aside time to pray, because there's no other way."

Ah. I was beginning to understand. However, understanding and liking were two different things. I was wishing there was another way, because I was afraid he was going to suggest I kneel for hours in a stuffy old church.

Or sit cross-legged while burning incense and repeating meaningless incantations. Now seemed like a good time to mount a bit of defense.

Chapter 53

IN DEFENSE OF
SELF-ABSORPTION

C amino, I like you," I began. "I really do. And I believe
I understand where you're coming from. But I don't
do well with sitting still. Never have; probably never
will. I'm pretty sure if I were a kid today, I'd be put on some
drug for ADHD. Besides that, I hate silence. God gave us a
mouth so we can talk."

"Before you go flying off the handle, let me get to my
point," Camino said patiently. Today he was also enjoying

a slice of blueberry pie. I'd declined. I was supposed to be suffering, right? "You're probably right. Let's be realistic. It's probably too much to ask for you to be still for an hour a day."

What the heck? An *hour*? I started to rise from my seat, but Camino gestured with his fork. "C'mon, Cleve, I'm messing with you," he chuckled. "Although you may some day work up to a couple of 30-minute prayer sessions a day, we are clearly not going to start there. You'd end up discouraged before you began and this whole exercise would be over. We definitely don't want that."

"Okay, I'll hear you out," I said suspiciously. I was on guard now, but I'd try to remain calm, because I really did like Camino, and I found I'd come to look forward to our weekly meetings.

"The key is to ease into the process, make it a habit, see the results and then decide if a little more time could be spent in prayer," Camino said simply.

I was processing that information when he switched gears a bit. "Do you ever read books, Cleve?"

"Well, yes, I do."

"Have you been able to maintain your concentration for five minutes or so?" Now he was zeroing in on his main pitch. I felt like we were playing salesman and client again. I figured I'd play along.

"Yes, Camino, I have." I knew what he was trying to do. I knew every trick in the book. Get the other person to say yes to something and it will be harder for him to say no later when it's time to close the deal.

"Many men and women who have had fantastic relationships with God have had trouble focusing or getting started in prayer," Camino said. "It's normal to feel a little awkward at first. Believe me, you wouldn't be the only one who didn't know how to get started with prayer. How did they overcome their difficulties? They used a good book as a spiritual primer to fuel the fire and keep them focused. As you will see the point of prayer is of course not to read the whole time. But a book can be very effective in helping you start and then stay on task while praying."

"What, you mean like the Bible?" I felt like a smart aleck when I said that.

"Well, of course, the Bible is great, but it could be any solid spiritual book," Camino said. "I'd like to share a technique with you that's been around for centuries. And again, I'm not expecting you to sit with a book praying for an hour a day. Do you think ten minutes a day would be doable?"

Now I'd look like a wimp if I said I thought I couldn't handle sitting still for a mere ten minutes, so I quickly agreed. Then I realized if I didn't hit the snooze button but simply kept my alarm set to the normal time, I'd have an extra twenty minutes every morning. Or eighteen to be exact, speaking in nine-minute increments.

"You do realize up until now, there has been virtually no prayer in my life at all," I reminded him.

"I know, you've said so," Camino said. "It's interesting, Cleve, because the traditions of constant and consistent prayer don't seem to be as strong as they used to be. Now is not the time to lecture on why this is, but fortunately many people are gravitating toward these traditions."

"Really? More people are praying?" I was skeptical. This whole thing sounded like hocus-pocus, but I was trying to keep an open mind, because so far, Camino's advice had actually had a positive effect on my life, without a ton of effort on my part and much to my surprise.

"Yes, but with the advances in technology and science and the removal of God from many public arenas, it's often difficult for young men and women to keep their faith. It's very easy to get caught up in chasing shallow dreams. And then, sadly, many lose their way, assuming they were even on a path of consistent prayer in the first place." He polished off his pie.

"So, are you asking me to pray with my family or alone?" I was a bit afraid of what his answer might be.

"Yes," he said simply. "Both. Let's explore this a bit."

Chapter 54

FAMILY AND PERSONAL PRAYER

I tapped my glass when the server looked our way, and she nodded, coming by to refill my water. I thanked her, and she moved off to another table.

"There's a very simple way to add prayer within your family," Camino said. "Prayer before meals is most common."

"Yeah, actually my wife does get us to do that sometimes," I said. "But it doesn't really mean anything."

"Of course it does. All prayer matters. And all prayers are heard. But here's an important point: I am guessing you haven't been paying attention to the words you are saying when you pray. Is this true?"

At my nod, he moved on. "Okay, that can be a simple fix. If it feels like something perfunctory, then you need to step back and pay attention to what you are saying and fully realize the importance of the words you are speaking. You could also consider adding special intentions from Cindy or the kids. Or just let them all know something important you have going on needs their prayers. Family dinnertime should ideally be a time of peace, checking in, mutual understanding, and support regarding what each member is going through at the time. I know this might sound farfetched to you, but it's possible to make great strides in this direction and to increase the value of your time together. If you are willing to make a few changes for the better."

"Okay, I think I know what I can do," I agreed. Maybe this wouldn't be so bad.

"The other most common times to pray as a family are after meals, in the morning, which is called morning offering in some traditions, and at night before bed. These can help to anchor your children, giving them an understanding that there's more to this world than what their immediate senses might indicate," Camino continued.

"Wow, that's a lot of prayer," I said. "I think they might put up a fight if I wanted them to pray with me that much."

"You might be pleasantly surprised, Cleve, but I'm not suggesting you go all or none," Camino said. "Start simply.

Make your mealtime prayer consistent. Do that for a while; then add prayer at night before the kids go to bed. Of course, this means you usually should be there when they are going to bed." He winked at me.

I nodded ruefully. Ouch.

"Some traditions have daily church services, and others customarily make short prayers during the late evening hours to reflect over one's day and express thanks for the wins, sorrow for the sins, and resolutions for the next day," Camino continued. "In fact, this latter practice can be incredibly powerful. However, all of this may be too much too soon for you so let's take a gradual approach. I suggest you anchor in your mealtime prayers and then focus mainly on prayer alone. By the way, some people call this meditation."

I knew it. Here's where the incense and chanting starts. I rolled my eyes, but I was surprised when Camino snapped his fingers.

"Focus, Cleveland," he said, his tone sharp. "This is important. We are not talking about the 'losing yourself into nothingness' meditation. We are talking about a meditation with the goal of walking closer to God. Ideally, this means dialogue. And while all forms of meditation have merit, this kind is potentially more powerful and more beneficial. We're going to start with a technique called *lectio divina* in Latin. It means 'divine reading,' and it's an excellent way to begin understanding the power and importance of prayer."

"Man, I thought I'd never have to learn another Latin phrase," I protested. "I actually took Latin in high school because I thought I wanted to be a doctor. While I never got that medical degree, it helped with the SAT and occasionally with literary references, but it never lived up to the importance my high school teacher ascribed to it."

"There's always something to be gained by learning any new language," Camino agreed. "With this technique, there are four steps, and I'm going to add a fifth bonus step. But first, we need to decide what source you will derive your prayer from. Since you are a Christian, I would recommend reading from the Bible to start. Specifically the New Testament."

"I haven't cracked a Bible in I don't know how long," I admitted sheepishly.

"Well, there are other books that can be used, but the Bible is likely the best for starting out," Camino said. "Also, you need to find a quiet place where you will not be interrupted. Some people go to a church; some wait until everyone else is in bed and close themselves in a home office. Once you establish the place and time, begin with a short prayer asking God for your upcoming prayer time to be fruitful. Then, it's time to dig in."

"Wait, I'm supposed to pray about my prayer time? That's kind of funny," I said. Again, Camino nailed me with that look, and I tucked my head in a rare act of submission.

Chapter 55
The Steps to Lectio Divina

Here are the official steps:

1. *Lectio*: To read. This is where you read a passage or two, even just a paragraph. Slowly. With intention. And often you may need to go over the same sentence two or three times to be sure you understand what it is about. Some people read over the same passage four times, with each repetition a chance to focus on a different word or inflection point. The goal is to see if anything begins to resonate with you.

2. *Meditatio*: To meditate. As you ponder the words, you don't want to overanalyze things. This is more about listening

to see if something, or someone, is speaking to you through the words. I know this may sound a bit odd, but once you try it a few times, I think you'll understand what I mean. The key is to enter into and experience the words.

3. *Oratio*: To pray. Again, since you are a Catholic Christian, your tradition tells you that prayer is a dialogue with God. So this step is all about listening. And you have the aid of the passage you just read to facilitate this.

4. *Contemplatio*: To contemplate. This is the hardest step, and one—truth be told—that is most rarely achieved. This is where you become virtually one with God. You and God become united, and love is what sustains it. We will likely come back to this as we move forward. For now, it's important to concentrate on the first three steps and consider this a bonus if it were to occur.

Now, as previously mentioned, some consider there to be a fifth step:

5. *Actio*: To take action. All prayer could lead to new actions, also known as resolutions. I would suggest it is important to take something away from your prayer that you want to work on. Besides being thankful for the time, of course."

My brain was overloaded. Somewhere in the middle of all of the explanation, I'd pulled out my phone and I was typing hastily in my favorite note-taking app. I'd gotten the words down, but I was afraid I was missing an explanation here or there. Fortunately Camino later provided me with a simple document to reference.

"So, what do you think?"

Chapter 56

HESITANT, BUT INTRIGUED

I think it's a lot to take in," I said truthfully. "Seems complicated, and time consuming. I don't see how I can fit all this into my day, much less into ten minutes."

"That's the interesting part, Cleve," Camino responded. "All I suggest you begin with is just ten minutes. It's simpler than you think. Basically all you are doing is reading, pondering, listening, and then seeing if anything sticks in terms of a resolution. Then, you move on to the next passage.

Beginners typically get through four or five passages in one ten-minute session, so it's not like you spend an hour on the same passage. More advanced people may stick with one passage for the whole ten minutes, or even for thirty minutes, but it just depends on what you feel you are getting from it and your reaction to it."

"Okay, so I guess this is where the 'just do it' part comes in," I said hesitantly. "I still don't see how this is going to work, but you haven't steered me wrong so far. I'll give it a shot."

Chapter 57

FINAL WORDS
OF WISDOM

reat!" Camino seemed genuinely pleased again. "One more tip: Put your daily prayer on your calendar, and then just like any other appointment, don't be a no-show. After all, this meeting is with God!"

"Ha!" I chuckled. "I never thought of it that way. But then again, I've never thought much about praying at all."

"Like I said before, unfortunately many people don't," Camino said. "It's a shame. But here's the amazing thing: If you follow what I have suggested and make prayer a part of your daily routine, you will find what many have found before. Prayer is our greatest weapon in the battle to be successful husbands, fathers, workers, and ultimately better men. Plus, it is absolutely necessary in order to experience authentic joy. I know we've been over this a few times. And the reason is hopefully becoming clearer to you- this is why you and I are talking in the first place."

I was scratching my head now. And truth be told, my brain hurt. It had been too long since I gave it a good workout.

"Well, I think I've overwhelmed you," Camino said with a smile. "More on joy when we meet next week. I suggest starting with the following Bible passage, but feel free to open it up anywhere and begin. Matthew 5, 6, and 7 are great, as is Mark 4."

I hastily scribbled the references down, not even sure what he meant by 5, 6, and 7. It couldn't be the page numbers. I'd figure it out later. First I'd have to find my Bible. I had no clue where it even was.

"Okay, I've got them all down, Camino," I said, folding up my napkin and placing it inside my inner jacket pocket. "I think I'm set. Thanks. I think."

"My pleasure, Cleve," Camino answered. "This might be the most important week of your life."

"Oh great, no pressure, right?" We finally shared a laugh.

"Truthfully, there is no pressure," Camino said reassuringly. "I just wanted you to know this week may seem trivial, but it's actually what I've been hoping to teach you all along. We have been building toward this. However, you wouldn't have been ready for it if I'd asked you to give prayer a shot the first week."

It was like he could truly read my mind, because I was just about to ask why he hadn't just cut to the chase and started there. Amazing!

"That's true," I agreed. As we walked toward the exit, I realized I had forgotten to pick up the tab. Laughing to myself, I returned to the table, paid the bill and left a nice tip for our patient server.

Chapter 58

CLEVE THE MONK

Okay, I know what you're going to think when I tell you what happened. You're going to say I shirked my duty, slacked off, whatever. And you'd be right. But in my defense, it's really, really hard for me, especially as a business owner, to set aside ten minutes for anything. Let alone something that requires being quiet. So, I'm sorry, but I only "prayed"—if you can even call it that—three times the whole week.

For the first four days I thought a lot about it, and I believe that has to count for something, seeing as how I'd never given prayer a thought before. And I really did try to fit it in, but it wasn't until the fifth day that I actually captured a quiet ten minutes. And that first time was just okay. Not great, but I will say it was peaceful, if for no other reason than it was ten minutes of quiet and reflection. He'd said I could start anywhere in the Bible, but I went with one of his suggestions and it was, well, interesting.

But the next day I decided to venture out on my own. I flipped open to the middle of my Bible and did one of those "close your eyes and point" things, where I decided to read whatever my finger landed on. And I got lucky with Psalm 51. In fact you might say I struck gold. I read it, and I have to say I feel silly saying this, but it really hit me. I mean seriously.

My Bible had a little intro that said it was the psalm of sorrow and repentance that David wrote after committing adultery and murder. I'd heard of David, as in David and Goliath, before, so I was intrigued. All I'd ever heard about him was that he was a really great king—someone God chose or something like that. How could he screw up this badly?

I know I'm not religious, but I just have to share the passage that really hit me. "Create a clean heart in me, O God; and renew a right spirit within me." For some reason, when I read this, some of the nasty things I'd done flooded through my mind. Yelling at Brian at the driving range. Sarcastic remarks I'd made to Cindy. Lies I'd told to clients and employees. I felt awful.

I remember thinking to myself, "Hey, I thought this was supposed to be making me feel better!" But then I couldn't help it. I felt *it* deep inside me, like maybe my heart or my soul? That sounds weird just saying it. I don't really even know what *it* is, but I felt this huge wave of sadness come over me. I could only describe it as something deeper than sadness. Sorrow? Yes, sorrow.

Now you might think that at this point I slammed my Bible shut and gave up. I don't need something to make me feel bad about myself. That happens often enough as it is! But no, I sat there for a moment, sort of wallowing in that crummy feeling, owning it. And suddenly, I felt a new wave washing over me. It was a relief—a sincere desire to be better. To do better. It's sounding strange, I know, but hang on. I'm getting to the good part.

I thought about how badly I wanted to be a good husband and father. No, not just good. I want to be a *great* father and husband. Not for myself, but for Jenna and Brian and Cindy. I have such a drive to win at work that it often consumes me. Business is tough. Owning a business is tougher yet. My family is counting on me, yes, but so are the families of everyone I employ. That's a lot of pressure.

That pressure builds and I feel like I need a stiff drink to relax before I go home to somehow take off the battlefield edge that is often appropriate for work but ill-suited for the family. I don't want to unload all that pressure on Cindy or the kids. But then I realized the time I spend at Ted's really limits my time at home, and it usually puts me in a very sarcastic mood that affects my interactions with Cindy and the kids. I was a naysayer, what I most loathe and my attitude was usually terrible. Sure, I'd been a bit better lately, and Cindy seemed to show signs of warming up to the new me, but I knew I could do more. Be more. I'd been such a failure; I think I could only improve from the low point I was at before I met Camino. I owed it to Cindy and the kids.

You might think my effort at prayer descended in a negative spiral. But actually, pretty much the opposite happened. As I thought about my actions and the passage, it gave me hope. David was a great king. And here he was, pleading with God to give him another chance. I've been faithful to Cindy, and I've certainly never killed someone! I can't imagine how terrible I would feel if I'd done something like that. To think that David, a king, was on his knees, begging God to forgive him made my far lesser trials seem all the more correctable.

Wow. I certainly felt like I might just need a clean heart. A new start. Some of that "right spirit" David was talking about. I felt a yearning for it. And I know, I know, it may seem a bit far-fetched at this point. I get it. I do. But this was for real. I felt it, and I really wanted it. And then I was somehow able to push through my sense of sorrow and transition into a greater sense of hope where I was compelled to tell God how badly I'd screwed up. I mean, I guess he knew it all already, but I felt like I *had* to tell him. Not only did I feel I needed to tell him but I felt better, healed in a sense, for the telling.

Then I did something I'd never done before. I sincerely prayed, asking God for something, but not for my benefit. I asked him to help me not let my family down again. I did actually feel something like peace come over me. It was really strange, but fantastic at the same time. It was a unique, indescribable experience. Maybe this was what Camino had referred to as "supernatural," I don't know? But I knew one thing for sure. I wanted this feeling again. And again and again. My ten minutes were up, so I finished with a quick thanks for the time. I moved forward with my day, feeling like a brand-new man.

As you can probably guess, I couldn't control my newfound excitement, and the next morning I was actually excited to get back to the same spot with the same passage so I could recreate the experience. And you know what happened? Zip. Zilch. Nada. Nothing at all. I really didn't even feel as great as the first day. Did I dream it? Was yesterday just a fluke, or did God give me a teaser, a dialogue to keep me coming back for more?

If that was what he was trying to do, it worked. I was hopeful that I might experience that feeling again the next day, but still a bit doubtful. Which leads me to today. I was actually really glad today was my day to meet with Camino. I couldn't wait to share my experience with him. Plus, I hoped he could put everything into perspective.

Chapter 59

FINAL REPORT

So, how did it go?" Camino jumped right in as I sat down. He'd already started on his iced tea and there was a water ready for me. For some reason Cliff's was almost empty today.

"Pretty great. I mean, well, not so great at first. The first four days I actually bombed the whole thing," I admitted sheepishly. "I just couldn't fit the quiet time in those first few days. It proved to be more challenging than I thought it would.

And you know I love challenges, so I was determined not to give up."

"Yes, I know you love challenges, but don't beat yourself up about those first few days, Cleve," Camino said. "I told you it wouldn't be easy and you wouldn't just drop into this like you've been doing it all your life."

"Yeah, I really did get frustrated with myself when I couldn't seem to figure it out, but then I did find some time the day before yesterday, and that's where it all began," I said.

"Remember when we talked about there being only three things a human can do?" Camino looked at me.

"Ah . . . I think I remember that, but honestly, there's been so much new information it's all kind of a blur," I admitted.

"Fair enough," Camino said. "Think, feel, and act. Remember from our earlier lesson, these are the only three things a human can do. Stimulate your intellect with the thought of prayer, direct your passions toward it, and then execute on it. Sounds easy, but I know it's anything but simple. The common understanding has been it takes twenty-one days to form a habit. There has been considerable research recently indicating it actually takes closer to sixty days to form a habit. So don't lose steam. Simply set the goal now to have sixty talks with God in the next sixty days. So in roughly two months you could be well on your way."

"Wow. That *is* a long time."

"Keep up the routine as best as you can, but try not to get discouraged when you miss a day here and there. The key is to not get discouraged," Camino encouraged. "There's a tendency to fall off the cliff quickly when you experience an early loss in any battle you undertake. A simple example is seen in dieting, but we can apply it here as well. People who 'cheat' by eating one thing off the approved diet are likely to consider the whole day a complete loss, so they start eating everything under the sun. Let's apply this to prayer. Say you miss your time, and you're at the office when it first dawns on you. All is not lost, despite what the little devil on your shoulder is telling you. You don't have to scrap the whole day and determine to 'do better' tomorrow. Start anew in the next hour. Take corrective action immediately. Begin again. Don't wait a whole day to start over!"

"I get it," I said, his logic dawning upon me. "This happens to me all the time at Ted's. As soon as I have one drink and some munchies, I figure I've already stopped there instead of going home, so why not stay longer? Doesn't matter what type of drink, I find it hard to stop at one of anything. It's too easy to throw the towel in.

Now that I think of it, this happens at home, too. I walk in, Cindy and I get in a little fight and the night is lost. I go do my thing. She does hers. We never try to work past the initial disagreement anymore."

"Exactly," Camino said with a smile. "At the end of the day, the pleasures of eating and drinking things we love are very powerful and hard to curb. This is usually a good instinct because we need sustenance to survive. We need to eat. It's just that sometimes our portions get out of control. So it's good that you've already come to a place where you realize that.

And the same principles apply to relationships. Only now we are affecting others and not just ourselves. To forgive quickly. To humble ourselves in order to achieve peace. To not hold a grudge about disagreements. These are all very difficult to do, but in the end they are essential to healthy relationships and authentic joy. And how are these fueled? In others words, where do we receive the sustenance to accomplish these difficult feats? I am guessing you already know the answer. Perfect segue. Let's talk about your prayer time. How did it go?"

"Well, the first time was interesting," I said. "I mean, I read some good stuff in Matthew, like you'd suggested, but it wasn't anything too remarkable. But the second day, I actually just flipped my Bible open to the middle and decided to go with Psalm 51."

"Oh yes, David's sorrow," Camino said, nodding. "That's a great one."

"Well, I had an odd experience," I said slowly. "I've actually been excited and nervous all at the same time when I thought about telling you."

"Go on," he suggested. "I think I'm going to like what I hear." He sat back, enjoying a breadstick while I spun my tale.

"It kind of felt like I lost myself a little," I said. I rushed forward with the next few words. "I'm not saying I lost myself like I fell asleep or something. I mean I literally didn't realize where I was, and I felt like someone was there with me. It was weird, but it was very peaceful."

"Yes!" Camino dropped his breadstick and leaned forward. "Keep going, Cleve, and trust me, you're not going to tell me anything that will make me think you're off your rocker."

"Well, I felt so good yesterday that this morning I set everything up exactly the same, and I even read the same passage," I said. "I wanted to have the same experience, but there was nothing. I thought yesterday that I'd figured this praying thing out, but obviously I was wrong."

"No, no, no," Camino said, waving the breadstick in my face. "You weren't wrong! How are you feeling today then, after your meditation time this morning?"

"I feel let down," I admitted. "I really wanted it to happen again, and I know that is sort of funny coming from the guy who was so skeptical just last week, but I'm disappointed. Discouraged."

"No worries," Camino said. "I think you probably don't realize how fortunate you are."

Chapter 60

FROM DISAPPOINTMENT TO APPRECIATION

Fortunate? I feel like I'm losing my mind! I don't feel fortunate at all!"

"Many very disciplined and prayerful people have maintained a regimented daily prayer routine for years and yet have never experienced what you are describing," Camino said excitedly. "This is important for two reasons. First, I assure you that God showed you the power of prayer, that it *is* real and tangible. It was literally the presence of God you felt on a deeper level, and it should hopefully fuel your prayer habit. So don't feel funny about it at all. This was a gift. You've had an incredible experience."

Hmm . . . maybe I wasn't completely crazy after all. And if some of these bigwigs in the prayer world hadn't even had an experience like that, maybe I was doing something right. I focused back on Camino and realized he was moving on to point two.

"I need to tell you that you may never have quite that experience again," he said. At my crestfallen look, he hurried on. "Or, you never know, it may happen several more times in the next few months. The key is to let go. Don't expect or demand it. Don't focus on it as something you *need*, or *have* to have. Prayer is immensely beneficial no matter what feelings we receive or whether or not we 'feel' like we've been heard or are being spoken to. And there are many other ways we can feel God's presence. After all, he is always with us."

"But after a while, if I don't get that feeling, I think I'll lose interest," I said honestly.

"The key is to be faithful in your struggle to form the habit and keep the dialogue going as best as you can. Plus, continue reminding yourself to believe in the truth that prayer really is the key to authentic joy. I'm repeating myself, but this is so important. Prayer is the greatest weapon we have in our fight to be virtuous as well as the greatest nourishment for our souls. Just like we can't neglect our bodies, we can't neglect our souls either. Failing to provide proper sustenance for our souls is the fastest way to undermine the presence of peace and joy in our lives."

"I guess I can see that, but this may be harder than I thought," I said.

"I mentioned last time we met that I would eventually cover why prayer leads to authentic joy, right?" Camino looked at me as if waiting for my permission to continue.

When I nodded, he launched into his explanation. "Here's my soapbox for the day. Many gurus tell you to seek pleasure and avoid pain. And while there is some merit here, we hopefully debunked this overly simplistic thought process with the time we spent with the Sisters. Pain is a reality of this world. But it can provide value when it is properly channeled."

"Yeah, they *did* seem very happy, even though they were quite skinny," I laughed.

"Then there are others who tell you the most important thing is to be physically fit, make tons of money, strive for total freedom or live for some earthly purpose," he continued. "And that's not all bad. It can get you pretty far, but only in worldly terms of power, money, and fame. None of these outcomes makes you truly happy."

"I don't know, I felt pretty happy the day I drove off the lot in my BMW," I said proudly.

"Sure, but did that happiness last?"

He had me there. No sooner had I bought my standard 5-series, my neighbor pulled into his driveway in a brand-new BMW M5. One-upped again. And then the first time I took the kids through a drive-through, of course thinking I looked cool to the kids in the window, I accidentally spilled the sundae container as I was passing it over to Brian. Not good. "I guess not," I admitted.

"You see this type of thing all the time with celebrities and executives who wake up one day and wonder what happened to their families, wives, kids, and everything they thought would always be there," Camino said.

"To some, sipping piña coladas on a beach provides the necessary satisfaction they believe they're seeking." I had to agree with that statement. I'd felt pretty happy on our honeymoon in France, just sitting on the banks of the Seine with Cindy, drinking red wine. Now I couldn't remember the last time I'd seen Cindy that happy, much less spending a relaxing evening with just her.

Camino pressed on. "Most of the people in search of pleasure through what money can buy are one mistake or one bad hire or just one economic turndown from losing everything," he said passionately. "And even if they didn't lose it all, they figure out eventually there is more to life than material things. Hopefully they realize the real pleasure and real beauty in life reside in those things that truly last forever. Like God. Our souls. Our families. Community. And even our legacy to an extent."

"I guess I can see that," I agreed. "There's been more than one point in our lives when we were one client away from losing the whole business, which would've cost us the house, our cars, pretty much everything."

"Yep," Camino said. "We want so badly to put everything in a box, to be in total control and play God. And we think we can figure everything out on our own. Here's an interesting question for you. Have you ever asked a scientist to measure a thought? Or love? Good luck with that. It can't be done. Not in any pure way. But we know these things exist. They are as real as anything physical. In fact, there is a branch of philosophy dedicated to understanding these truths. It's called metaphysics, which means literally 'the things after physics' or the science of transcending what is physical. Unfortunately many modern philosophers discount the truths inherent in this science and now is not the time to digress down this path. The most important takeaway is for you to understand what is obvious with common sense: Some things are hard to grasp, but are still real. Wouldn't you agree?"

"Well sure," I said.

"They can't be seen or measured in an empirical way because they have no physical substance in our world," Camino went on. "They are all part of divine nature, even, to use the phrase you find most annoying, they exist on a 'supernatural' plane. So, how do we bring more of this into our lives? More love, more God? The best way is through prayer."

Once again I was feeling overwhelmed, but this time I had a special notebook I had brought with me to take notes. I was also using it to keep track of my meditations. Camino had mentioned something about this in passing. I felt a little bit of pride mixed with humble bewilderment that I actually took action on one of his small suggestions.

"It's going to take me a while to unpack all of this, Camino," I said. "But I think I understand. As you've probably gathered, I'm not really a touchy-feely kind of guy. But through our time together you've somehow broken through my natural skepticism and helped me experience truths I never thought existed. Or maybe I knew them all along and you just helped me uncover them?"

"What I teach is written on every person's heart. And when you're applying these principles and seeing the results in person it's hard for you *not* to make positive strides," Camino agreed with a smile.

"Yeah, I guess these past few weeks have had a pretty big impact on me," I admitted. What an understatement, actually! This experience has taught me so much. I just hope the impact continues and that I stick to the habits I am beginning to form.

"I would certainly hope so," Camino said. "Keep in mind, we have plenty of time to talk about things like this in the future. For now, let's be thankful we've come this far together in a very short amount of time. It's only been three weeks since we started meeting."

"I know, it's pretty crazy," I said. "It seems like a lifetime ago. I really do owe you one, Camino. I know I've got a long way to go, but I've never felt more on the right track in my life. I'd never heard of some of these techniques before, and others are things you have reintroduced in a new way.

What shocks me most of all is that if someone had told me a month ago that I would be praying, by myself, in total silence and not just for something I wanted, I wouldn't have believed them for a second," I laughed.

"You *have* made some substantive changes in a short time," Camino agreed. "Let's raise a glass to that. To you, your progress, and to your family." He held up his tea. "May you make your home cheerful and God-centered while you strive to learn more truths, grow closer to God and continue your journey toward authentic joy."

"I'll drink to that!" I clinked glasses with him.

Chapter 61

REALITY CHECK

I 'm far from perfect though," I said. "I still like my car and Ted's and ball games and making money."

"Cleve, there's nothing wrong with liking those things. It's just that they can't be the top priorities in your life," Camino said. "We have to be careful not to let our pride get the better of us. As you may know, pride is the greatest of the seven deadly sins."

"Ooh. Sounds scary," I quipped.

"It can be. But no need to ponder that now. Or at least not yet," Camino said with a look on his face I had grown accustomed to. Deep in thought. Or maybe, now that I think of it, he was pausing to pray?

"Good," I said. "On another note, I would like to invite you to go to a ball game with me next weekend. I'm bringing the whole family. I was thinking I wouldn't tell them you're my mentor or anything. Just that you're a friend. I want them to meet you because you've had such an impact on my life and theirs, too. And, by the way, what do I owe you for all this?"

Camino was still thinking. He'd pursed his lips, so I waited. I knew something was coming down the pipeline, but I'd learned by now that he would introduce it when he was ready.

"You owe me three more meetings," he answered finally. "I do understand you have things left to improve. For instance, we all need to work on our pride constantly," Camino said thoughtfully. "But it's good that you shared your prayer experience and the little bit about your car and money, because now I have a solid sense of where we will go with our next session together . . . after I eat my blueberry pie and join you and your family at the ball game next weekend."

"So we're going to meet three more times?" I felt like a new man. I had no idea what else Camino could spring on me, but I'd figured I'd just keep working to improve on what I'd already learned.

"There's so much more, Cleve!"

"There's more?" Oh boy.

"There's always more," Camino said with a wink as he enjoyed his first bite of pie.

I wonder what he meant by "we all need to work on our pride constantly?" Guessing I have more challenges ahead. Batter up!

ABOUT THE AUTHOR

Avoiding nourishment for our souls is the fastest way
to invite a lack of peace and joy into our lives.
—**Camino**, *Rethink Happy*

Doug Kisgen is a serial entrepreneur, speaker, consultant, and personality expert. He has extensive experience in senior care, performing arts, and working with at-risk teenagers and entrepreneurs, which he's found to be very much alike! He has a Bachelor of Science in Biology, a Servant Leadership Certificate from Gonzaga Graduate School, is a certified catechist, and a graduate of the Entrepreneurial Masters Program hosted by MIT. He has also participated in formal spiritual direction and doctrinal formation since 2008.

Those are the credentials behind what Doug does, but his real drive comes from his desire to help others operate at the highest level possible, both in their personal and professional lives. His uncanny talent and experience have allowed him to assist many different people from various walks of life in the area of finding true happiness. This book combines his experiences with the practical application of the essential principles he's learned along the way.

Doug and his wife of twenty-plus years have five children and live in the hill country of South Texas.

ACKNOWLEDGMENTS

First of all, I give thanks to God. Secondly, my wife, Kate, my soul mate. Thirdly, my children, Cassandra, Alexander, Joseph, Olivia, and Thomas.

A very special thank you goes to Adrienne Lewis for making this manuscript truly shine. I would like to think the ideas were solid and some of the storylines were interesting, but the flow of the book and especially the dialogue left much to be desired before I handed it over to her. Adrienne added her pixie dust and made my "Pinocchio" book a "real" book, and so to her I am especially grateful. And now if I ever take full credit you will know why my nose grew! Ha. And while we are on the editing subject, I would like to thank Angie Kiesling and her crew at The Editorial Attic, Rev. William Shaughnessy for his edits and suggestions and finally a big thank you to

Wilbur Matthews who gave exceedingly of his time to improve the flow of the book. And finally a special thanks to David and everyone at Morgan James Publishing: thank you for believing in this project!

I would like to thank many others including family, friends, colleagues, and clients. You have all influenced me. I apologize in advance for anyone I accidentally omit or couldn't include given editing time constraints.

Jim, Jean, Darren and Lauren, Wendy, Reinhard, Terri (a blessed memory); Max and Jeannine (a blessed memory), Mike and Mary, Chris and Judith, Angela, Max and Sue, Tom, Rachel and James; ; Joey C., Nick, Tony, Abdul and families; the Little Sisters of the Lamb in KC (yes, they are real); Wayne and Jackie, plus the whole crew at The MAC, Cathy, Stacey and Chad, Suzanne, Tim, Heath, Holly, Phil, Marlys, and Delvin; Paul and Lori Hogan and all at Home Instead Senior Care; John, Dave, Jeff, Ryan, John, Sailynn; a hearty shout-out to the artists formerly known as Red Ellis—Larry, Byron, Lane, Kerry and Sherry; the inspirational hearts and souls at Boys Town; Brandon Henry; the Boyz—Pat, Tristin, Little Doug, Sean, Brandon, Chad, David, Nathan, Kelly, Ryan, Romaine, Ronnie, Trevor, and Bear; Gary and Cec at Culture Index for opening my eyes to the amazing world of applied behavioral psychology and Jason W.; all the crew in KC—Richard, Rob, Christopher, Boniface, Josh, Mike, John, David, Bo, Todd, Clem, Matt; Dieter (all three, but especially Mr. Sandman apostrophe) and Kathy, Brian, Michelle; the Entrepreneurs' Organization (EO), especially EO KC!—Mary, Mary "W", John "Dr. No", Reid "House", Luke and Linda, Peter, Austen, Todd, Mark; Alec,

Kirk, Ron, Ted, Gunner, Tim, Joe, Kelly, Chad, Michael, Josh, Michael, Chris, Jim, Tony, Joe, David, Jay, Tawnya, Matthew, Rajiv, Jim, Corey, Jimmy, William, Zach and Tina, Debbie, Jaime, Dave, Peter, Aaron, Steve, Joe, David, Lou, Adam, Frank, Renee, Florian, Amy, Matt, Matthew, Jim, Craig, Rob, Ken, Tim, Jared, Arnold, Phyliss, Andy, Laird, Brian, Travis, Theresa, Matt, Amy, Michael, Carmen, George and Yuri, Dan, Aaron, William, Gary, Stacey, Michele, Sarah, Chris, Gavin (2), Darlene, Joe P., Mike M., Jay and Ashlee, Deep Prime, Wilbur, Chad, Mike, Chris, Peter, Kevin, Shawn, Brett; SA crew, Jeff, Mark, Chad, Kevin, Armando, Paul, Gerard, Robert, Paul, Ted, Mike, Robert, Don, Richard, Sathesh; John, Jay, Jerry, Carlos, Jim, Peter, Mike, Javier and a special thanks to the 48 Days Mastermind and Dan Miller for his outstanding mentorship.

Keep the *Rethink Happy* Conversation Going!

If you are interested in learning more about the Rethink Happy movement for yourself or your organization, including speaking, coaching, and courses, please contact Kisgen Group, Inc. at the following:

Online: rethinkhappy.com
Email: doug@rethinkhappy.com

Be sure to sign up for Doug's videos and "rethoughtful" emails!

Camino mentions the need to **assess the talent** of any organization. If you are an entrepreneur/business owner, you can sign up for a free demonstration of the Culture Index program which includes survey results for you and a sampling of your current employees for FREE! Please go to kisgengroup.com to learn more.

CPSIA information can be obtained
at www.ICGtesting.com
Printed in the USA
LVOW12s1344230816

501507LV00005B/135/P